THE ART OF *praying* THE SCRIPTURES

A FRESH LOOK AT *LECTIO DIVINA*

JOHN PAUL JACKSON
WITH JOHN E. THOMAS

Table of Contents

FROM THE AUTHOR 1
CHAPTER 1
Lectio Divina in History 7
CHAPTER 2
Praying of the Scriptures Within the Scriptures 9
CHAPTER 3
Taking It Slow 13
CHAPTER 4
The Joy of Communion 15
CHAPTER 5
Discovering Renewed Fellowship 19
CHAPTER 6
Sharper Than any Two-Edged Sword 23
CHAPTER 7
The Underlying Spiritual Rhythm 25
CHAPTER 8
Friendship with God 29
CHAPTER 9
The Importance of Understanding the Scriptures 33
CHAPTER 10
Remaining in His Embrace 35
CHAPTER 11
The Rhythm of Spiritual Oscillation 39
CHAPTER 12
Four Stages of *Lectio Divina* 43
CHAPTER 13
The Nine Steps 45
CHAPTER 14
Preparing the Body and Soul 49
CHAPTER 15
Recognize God Wants to Commune with You 55
CHAPTER 16
Deep Listening: Hearing with the Ears of the Heart 57
CHAPTER 17
Read *and* Listen While Reading 59
CHAPTER 18
Intensive Prayer 61

CHAPTER 19

Contemplation 65

CHAPTER 20

Abiding 69

CHAPTER 21

Sealing the Moment—Journal 73

CHAPTER 22

Where Do I Begin? 75

CHAPTER 23

Lectio Divina in a Group Setting 79

CHAPTER 24

Make an Appointment with God 81

CHAPTER 25

The Practice of Desire, Discipline, and Delight 83

LECTIO DIVINA PRACTICE

85   The Art of Praying the Scriptures—Reference Card

86   Walking in the Light

90   Christ—the Word and the Light

94   Wisdom—Christ as Wisdom Personified

98   The Living Word and Great High Priest

102 The Father Chose Me as a Son

106 I am Filled, Circumcised, Buried, and Made Alive in Christ

110 Think on These Things

114 Counting All Things Loss to Know Him

118 The Lord Calls, Equips, Keeps, and Anoints—Declaring
     What Is to Come

122 God's Righteousness Through Faith

126 A Vision of the Throne of God

130 "I am Willing—Be Cleansed"

134 "Neither Do I Condemn You"

138 A Vision of the Risen Christ

142 Nothing Can Separate Me

146 Anointed for Purpose

150 The Winter Is Past

154 I Am a Partaker of the Divine Nature

158 I Will Do Greater Works Through the Love Jesus Shows Me

162 Don't Worry—Just Seek the Kingdom

166 Restore Me, O God!

172 About the Author

173 About the Contributing Author

Surely I have calmed and quieted my soul,
Like a weaned child with his mother;
Like a weaned child is my soul within me.
~ Psalm 131:2 (Amplified)

From the Author

OH, HOW I LOVE YOUR LAW!
I MEDITATE ON IT ALL DAY LONG.
~ PSALM 119:97

For more than two months, I read the eighth chapter of Proverbs ever day. I was inexplicably drawn to it. Every time I opened the Bible to read, I turned to that book and read that chapter over and over, as if I were trying to find a missing part or some mystery. I would usually end up reading the passage very slowly, often praying for understanding of what I was drawn to. Sometimes I took a week to read and focus on one single verse. Unknown to me at the time, in the process of all of this I was changed. Light seemed to enter me, my thoughts became sharper, my focus in life came to be precise, and God's plan in my reading that passage was accomplished.

While looking for answers to these types of spiritual riddles, I have discovered that something mysterious happens to and in us as we read through the Scriptures and pray in this fashion. You might say that this type of reading is almost like an art form, and the more often it is practiced, the deeper one experiences prayer and the Word of God. The ancients of the early Church called it *lectio divina*.

Lectio divina is Latin for "holy reading," meaning holy reading of the Scriptures. It is an ancient Christian spiritual discipline of reading and praying the Scriptures with focused intent. You cannot be impatient and read the Bible in this manner. This practice is the unhurried savoring of the text so the eternal truths contained therein enter our spirits, and with that entrance we are more than changed—we are transformed. The "unhurried savoring" is a very important aspect of the transformation process.

A literal translation of the Latin *lectio divina* could be rendered "divine choosings" since *lectio* comes from the root *lego*, which means "picking" or "choosing." This would suggest that, when praying God's Word back to Him, we're not simply connecting with a sacred text, but we are literally connecting with God Himself through His Word. If the Bible is truly a "living word," then this connection must be possible. Connection with the Bible is at the heart of this form of prayer, and it has been throughout the ages.

Prayer is the most mentioned doctrine and practice in Scripture. The command to pray is found 250 times in the Bible. In addition, praying specific prayers is mentioned another 280 times. The Bible is full of examples of godly men and women whose lives were infused and nations changed by prayer.

It is essential to learn not only our need to pray but also the results of prayer, the nature of prayer, and that the deeper types of prayer require giving God our full attention as we pray.

Giving God our full attention, especially in this hurried age, can be extremely difficult. There are noises all around us—cell phones and iPads ringing, text notifications, Twitter and Facebook notifications, along with dozens of other updates and new service announcements.

Lectio divina is a way to practice giving God your full, undivided attention. The more you practice this method of reading the Scriptures, the easier it becomes to focus on God without the distractions of the day trying to take over your consciousness. Still, it does often require us to turn off the sound on our cell phones, notepads, laptops, and computers to ensure that what we want to focus on remains our focus.

Lectio divina is slowly and deliberately praying the Scriptures, thereby allowing God to speak to you through them. In so doing, His Spirit connects to your spirit, and in that interior connection transformation accelerates. In some parallel spiritual way, God once again breathes the light of His Word into our spirits. That which was dormant comes alive. That which was languishing becomes vibrant once again.

You will find that this book reads very slowly. This was done purposefully to help slow you down and prepare you for this kind of prayer. Carve out some time and put the brakes on the fast pace of life around you. Find a place of silence and wait before the Lord.

For some, the isolation of this type of reading prayer is too much to take on at first. Some prefer to have other like-minded "pray-ers" around to encourage each other. There is an aspect of *lectio divina* that is good when practiced in small groups. For those of you who do not feel comfortable in isolated prayer times, here's a way to begin *lectio divina* in a small group setting.

Find a short passage of Scripture that speaks to you and those near you. Make enough photocopies of the passage to hand out to your circle of friends. Begin with individual meditation or silent prayer on that passage.

At a point when the Holy Spirit prompts, one member of the circle reads the passage aloud. Just listen like you would listen to any story. Try to let go of any preconceived ideas you have about whatever passage you're using. Listen with your heart and your head.

Another member of the circle reads the same passage aloud a second time. This time, listen for one word or phrase that reaches out to you. After the second reading is finished, wait until the Holy Spirit moves you, and if He does, simply say that word or phrase out loud quietly.

After a short period of silence, have another member of your small group read the passage a third time. This time, members of the circle are given the opportunity to explain in a brief and prayerful fashion what the passage taught them about God, themselves, or the spiritual search they have been on.

Don't allow this to become a discussion or a debate; it is a time of disclosure, not argument. Try to listen deeply as each one speaks. Listen with your spirit to empathize with that person and the spiritual journey he or she has been on. Be open for a possible moment of grace when the Holy Spirit might say, "This is for you."

This method of *lectio divina* ends with a fourth reading of the passage. You might notice the reading sounds a bit different to you than it did before, or that it means more now than the first time you heard it.

This is when the Scripture and you become one; it is also when transformation begins. True, there are deeper realms to be found, but the initial phase begins here.

Listening to God begins with consciously centering on Him and resting in His presence. We reject the dictates of our souls to connect in spirit-to-Spirit communion. The desire to commune with God is just one part of the human spirit. The spirit is three parts: wisdom, communion, and conscience. Intentional centering on God is to engage your spirit in unhindered focus on Him. God is looking for those who worship Him in spirit and in truth. Thus, listening to Him begins with the spiritual element of communion.

> FOR THUS SAYS THE LORD GOD,
> THE HOLY ONE OF ISRAEL:
> "IN RETURNING AND REST YOU SHALL BE SAVED;
> IN QUIETNESS AND CONFIDENCE
> SHALL BE YOUR STRENGTH."
> ~ ISAIAH 30:15

Throughout this book, we will go over the place *lectio divina* has in Christian history and where we find evidence for it in the Scriptures. Next, I will discuss the principle of taking it slow when praying in this way. Here, in your quiet place, you will uncover the truth of what the prophet Isaiah wrote, that strength is found in quietness.

You will learn how you are invited into joyful communion with the Father, how the Father desires renewed fellowship with you. You will also discover how you can enter into a divine rhythm that draws you closer to Him and, in so doing, how you maintain friendship with God and remain in His embrace.

As the book progresses, I will give you some practical steps for entering into this time of prayer.

John Paul Jackson

HEAR, O LORD, WHEN I CRY WITH MY VOICE!
HAVE MERCY ALSO UPON ME, AND ANSWER ME.
WHEN YOU SAID, "SEEK MY FACE,"
MY HEART SAID TO YOU,
"YOUR FACE, LORD, I WILL SEEK."
-PSALM 27:7-8

LECTIO DIVINA IN HISTORY

Lectio divina is rooted deeply in Christian history. During the Middle Ages, monks would use the Psalms as inspiration for the practice of *lectio divina*. Though it was largely ignored until the early 1900s, within the last twenty years individuals have revisited this ancient method of prayer and contemplation that Christians used for centuries.

> LORD, YOU HAVE BEEN OUR DWELLING PLACE IN ALL GENERATIONS. BEFORE THE MOUNTAINS WERE BROUGHT FORTH, OR EVER YOU HAD FORMED THE EARTH AND THE WORLD, EVEN FROM EVERLASTING TO EVERLASTING, YOU ARE GOD.
> ~ PSALM 90:1-2

Historically, those who sought a deeper spiritual path meditated on and prayed the Scriptures—not to gain knowledge or gather information but to become "one spirit" with the Living God. They believed the Bible to really be a living Word that would activate their spirits and attune them to anything the Spirit of God might want to teach them about the Creator.

In morning and evening prayer, monks would gather together and sing or pray the Psalms. In addition at different times during the day, they would make place for solitude and silence and practice *lectio divina*.

From the early Church fathers forward, there were many individuals in Christian history who employed this method of praying the Scriptures. Not only did they pray the Scriptures themselves, but they taught those under them the art of *lectio divina*. Tertullian in the late second century, Bernard of Clairvaux, Julian of Norwich, St. John of the Cross, Madame Jeanne Guyon, and John Calvin are some names in Christian history you may recognize, and each of these men and women espoused prayer in this fashion.

While much of Europe plunged into the Dark Ages after the collapse of Rome, monks in Ireland stood out as beacons of God's light. They prayed the Psalms every dawn and sunset and practiced devotional reading of the Scriptures throughout their day. Rooted in this spiritual mindset, this tiny country sent out missionaries across Europe to preach the gospel and remind people to worship Christ, instead of returning to the ways of pagan worship practiced by their ancestors.

St. John of the Cross worked with St. Teresa of Avila to restore purity to monastic orders in the vicinity of Avila, Spain, during the sixteenth century. Both of them taught the men and women under them to spend many hours of their day in biblical devotional reading and *lectio divina*.

The Moravians, who lived at Herrnhut in Germany during the eighteenth century, started a prayer meeting that lasted one hundred years. From this prayer meeting came the modern missions movement. One of the ways they prayed during this incredible meeting of continuous prayer was the devotional reading and praying of the Scriptures.

We can also see glimpses of this kind of prayer in the Bible during David's reign as king, as we will discuss in the next chapter.

STAND UP AND BLESS THE LORD YOUR GOD
FOREVER AND EVER!

BLESSED BE YOUR GLORIOUS NAME,
WHICH IS EXALTED ABOVE ALL BLESSING AND PRAISE!
YOU ALONE ARE THE LORD;
YOU HAVE MADE HEAVEN,
THE HEAVEN OF HEAVENS, WITH ALL THEIR HOST,
THE EARTH AND EVERYTHING ON IT,
THE SEAS AND ALL THAT IS IN THEM,
AND YOU PRESERVE THEM ALL.
THE HOST OF HEAVEN WORSHIPS YOU.
~ NEHEMIAH 9:5-6

PRAYING OF THE SCRIPTURES WITHIN THE SCRIPTURES

Moses used the entire book of Deuteronomy to build the people up in the Lord by repeating and reiterating the things they already knew. Through Moses, the Lord commanded the people to meditate on what they had learned and teach it to their children.

THE LAW OF YOUR MOUTH IS BETTER TO ME THAN THOUSANDS OF COINS OF GOLD AND SILVER.
~ PSALM 119:72

AND THESE WORDS WHICH I COMMAND YOU TODAY SHALL BE IN YOUR HEART. YOU SHALL TEACH THEM DILIGENTLY TO YOUR CHILDREN, AND SHALL TALK OF THEM WHEN YOU SIT IN YOUR HOUSE, WHEN YOU WALK BY THE WAY, WHEN YOU LIE DOWN, AND WHEN YOU RISE UP.
~ DEUTERONOMY 6:6-7

In the tabernacle of David, those who were selected to minister in song and music had to be at least thirty years of age and also had to be well versed in the Torah (see 1 Chronicles 23). One can easily assume from reading through Psalm 78, Psalm 105, or many other psalms that those times of prayer and praise in the tabernacle involved praying the ancient Scriptures and, in so doing, reminding ourselves of His promises to us. Here's a portion of Psalm 105 as an example:

HE REMEMBERS HIS COVENANT FOREVER,
THE WORD WHICH HE COMMANDED, FOR A THOUSAND GENERATIONS,
THE COVENANT WHICH HE MADE WITH ABRAHAM,

AND HIS OATH TO ISAAC,
AND CONFIRMED IT TO JACOB FOR A STATUTE,
TO ISRAEL AS AN EVERLASTING COVENANT,
SAYING, "TO YOU I WILL GIVE THE LAND OF CANAAN
AS THE ALLOTMENT OF YOUR INHERITANCE,"
WHEN THEY WERE FEW IN NUMBER,
INDEED VERY FEW, AND STRANGERS IN IT.
~ PSALM 105:8-12

So we see even within the Scriptures that people practiced praying God's Word and meditated on it.

The word *selah*, which is difficult to translate into English, carries the idea of pausing to meditate, pray, and personally apply what you just heard or read. Here is an example from Psalm 24:10:

WHO IS THIS KING OF GLORY?
THE LORD OF HOSTS,
HE IS THE KING OF GLORY. SELAH

Once you hear or read *selah*, the thought is that you would pause to meditate on both the question and the answer. Who is this King of glory? He is not just a king but the King of glory. Then you ask more questions: "Lord, what is meant by glory? Lord, will You show me a revelation of You as King?" Then you wait to hear, and you begin to meditate on the answer revealed in the text: The Lord of hosts—*He* is the King of glory. Now ask yourself, "What does *that* mean?" He has a myriad of angelic, spiritual beings ready to do His bidding. "Lord, why do You choose to reveal Yourself as the Lord of hosts in this passage?"

All of these unpacking questions can be asked as we read and pray through the Psalms—indeed, as we pray through all the Scriptures. That is at the heart of what *selah* means.

In the Psalms, we see how David regularly reminded God of the great things He did in Israel's history and in his own personal history. These prayers had tremendous power as he recalled the multi-layered promises of God.

> REMEMBER, O LORD, YOUR TENDER MERCIES AND
> YOUR LOVINGKINDNESSES,
> FOR THEY ARE FROM OF OLD.
> DO NOT REMEMBER THE SINS OF MY YOUTH, NOR MY
> TRANSGRESSIONS;
> ACCORDING TO YOUR MERCY REMEMBER ME,
> FOR YOUR GOODNESS' SAKE, O LORD . . .
> KEEP MY SOUL, AND DELIVER ME;
> LET ME NOT BE ASHAMED, FOR I PUT MY TRUST IN YOU.
> ~ PSALM 25:6-7, 20

Psalm 89, composed by Ethan the Ezrahite, is another example of recalling God's promises in the Scriptures and history and then asking Him to fulfill His promise in that day:

> O LORD GOD OF HOSTS,
> WHO IS MIGHTY LIKE YOU, O LORD?
> YOUR FAITHFULNESS ALSO SURROUNDS YOU.
> YOU RULE THE RAGING OF THE SEA;
> WHEN ITS WAVES RISE, YOU STILL THEM.
> YOU HAVE BROKEN RAHAB IN PIECES, AS ONE WHO IS SLAIN;
> YOU HAVE SCATTERED YOUR ENEMIES WITH YOUR MIGHTY ARM.
>
> THEN YOU SPOKE IN A VISION TO YOUR HOLY ONE,
> AND SAID: "I HAVE GIVEN HELP TO ONE WHO IS MIGHTY;
> I HAVE EXALTED ONE CHOSEN FROM THE PEOPLE.
> I HAVE FOUND MY SERVANT DAVID;
> WITH MY HOLY OIL I HAVE ANOINTED HIM,
> WITH WHOM MY HAND SHALL BE ESTABLISHED;
> ALSO MY ARM SHALL STRENGTHEN HIM.
> LORD, WHERE ARE YOUR FORMER LOVINGKINDNESSES,
> WHICH YOU SWORE TO DAVID IN YOUR TRUTH?
> REMEMBER, LORD, THE REPROACH OF YOUR SERVANTS—
> HOW I BEAR IN MY BOSOM THE REPROACH OF
> ALL THE MANY PEOPLES,
> WITH WHICH YOUR ENEMIES HAVE REPROACHED, O LORD,
> WITH WHICH THEY HAVE REPROACHED THE FOOTSTEPS OF YOUR
> ANOINTED.
> ~ PSALM 89:8-10, 19-21, 49-51

In the New Testament we find many references to people singing psalms. While some people at that time may have been doing simple reciting, we can glean from the passages that this singing of Scripture was a form of praying the Scriptures. Here are some examples:

> AND WHEN THEY HAD SUNG A HYMN,
> THEY WENT OUT TO THE MOUNT OF OLIVES.
> ~ MARK 14:26

This hymn was probably one of or all the Psalms of Ascents (Psalms 120–134):

> BUT AT MIDNIGHT PAUL AND SILAS WERE PRAYING AND
> SINGING HYMNS TO GOD, AND THE PRISONERS WERE
> LISTENING TO THEM.
> ~ ACTS 16:25

Again, this "hymn" probably was from the book of Psalms:

> BE FILLED WITH THE SPIRIT, SPEAKING TO ONE ANOTHER
> IN PSALMS AND HYMNS AND SPIRITUAL SONGS,
> SINGING AND MAKING MELODY IN YOUR HEART TO THE
> LORD, GIVING THANKS ALWAYS FOR ALL THINGS TO GOD
> THE FATHER IN THE NAME OF OUR LORD JESUS CHRIST.
> ~ EPHESIANS 5:18B-20

"He arose at four o'clock in the morning, and throwing himself before the mercy-seat, for three hours wrestled with God in mighty prayer . . . Immediately after breakfast and family worship he would again retire with his Bible into his study, and spend until near noon in the same hallowed employment. Here unquestionably was the great secret of his power in public prayer and in preaching. The Lord who sees in secret, rewarded him openly. Every sermon was sanctified by prayer."

John Smith
Written by David Smithers

Taking it Slow

Lectio divina is about taking it slow. Let's do an exercise of slow reading here. We will start with a familiar passage: John 1. Look at verses 1, 4, 9, and 14, and slowly and deliberately pray through them:

> LET THE WORDS OF MY MOUTH AND THE MEDITATION OF MY HEART BE ACCEPTABLE IN YOUR SIGHT, O LORD, MY STRENGTH AND MY REDEEMER.
> ~ PSALM 19:14

¹IN THE BEGINNING WAS THE WORD, AND THE WORD WAS WITH GOD, AND THE WORD WAS GOD.

⁴IN HIM WAS LIFE, AND THE LIFE WAS THE LIGHT OF MEN.

⁹THAT WAS THE TRUE LIGHT WHICH GIVES LIGHT TO EVERY MAN COMING INTO THE WORLD.

¹⁴AND THE WORD BECAME FLESH AND DWELT AMONG US, AND WE BEHELD HIS GLORY, THE GLORY AS OF THE ONLY BEGOTTEN OF THE FATHER, FULL OF GRACE AND TRUTH.

This passage is full of grace and truth. Jesus is the Word, and the Word—the Bible—is written through and from Him, inspired by the Holy Spirit. *Lectio Divina*, then, is speaking and breathing the light of His Word as we contemplate His glory.

When we gaze in this way at the risen Christ, it produces a spiritual transformation within us. We are then changed into what we behold.

I often tell people, "What you focus on is what you make room for." Behold the Lord—focus on the Lord, and you will make room for the Lord. The apostle Paul explains this very principle in 2 Corinthians 3:18a: "But we all, with unveiled face, beholding as in a mirror the glory of the Lord, are being transformed." Beholding the glory of God transforms us; we are "being transformed into the same image from glory to glory."

In order to enter into this posture of beholding the Lord, we need to calm and quiet our souls, as the Psalmist talks about in Psalm 131:2:

> SURELY I HAVE CALMED AND QUIETED MY SOUL,
> LIKE A WEANED CHILD WITH HIS MOTHER;
> LIKE A WEANED CHILD IS MY SOUL WITHIN ME.

Remember that Jesus said, "Assuredly, I say to you, unless you are converted and become as little children, you will by no means enter the kingdom of heaven. Therefore whoever humbles himself as this little child is the greatest in the kingdom of heaven." So calm and quiet your soul like a weaned child while you seek to posture yourself for prayer. I will give recommendations on how to do this in later chapters.

Take it slow while you prayerfully, deliberately begin to read through the Scriptures. Don't worry if you spend a month or two in a single chapter of the Bible. If that is where you are beholding the Lord, and if that is where He is speaking to you, stay there until He moves you to a different chapter. You will find it is important not to move on to another verse until the Spirit of God moves.

THE JOY OF COMMUNION

Beholding the Lord through *lectio divina* is an intimate form of communion. Communion comes from the two words *common* and *union*. When we celebrate the Lord's Supper—communion—by taking

IN YOUR PRESENCE IS FULLNESS OF JOY; AT YOUR RIGHT HAND ARE PLEASURES FOREVER MORE.
~ PSALM 16:11B

the bread and wine in faith, we come into union, or *communion*, with the Lord, our Savior. We take communion in remembrance of Him and His work on the Cross. He actively invites us into this union, and when we respond, we come into union with the Light of the World and the light of His Word.

John 8:12 speaks of coming into union with the Light of the World:

THEN JESUS SPOKE TO THEM AGAIN, SAYING, "I AM THE LIGHT OF THE WORLD. HE WHO FOLLOWS ME SHALL NOT WALK IN DARKNESS, BUT HAVE THE LIGHT OF LIFE."

First John 1:7 states the same thing with additional revelation:

BUT IF WE WALK IN THE LIGHT AS HE IS IN THE LIGHT, WE HAVE FELLOWSHIP WITH ONE ANOTHER, AND THE BLOOD OF JESUS CHRIST HIS SON CLEANSES US FROM ALL SIN.

God is light, and God is love; therefore, love is God's light. If we love people, then we cannot help but radiate that light. It is very simple: if you don't love people, you will not radiate that spiritual light, but if you do love people, you will radiate that light. As we seek fellowship with God, we enter His light. When He comes into us and dwells in us, we begin to radiate that light and His love to people around us.

Love is one of the nine fruits of the Spirit. Whenever we encounter the God-breathed Word of God, we can seek out the particular fruit of the Spirit the Lord is demonstrating to us. The nine fruits of the Spirit are love, joy, peace, patience, kindness, goodness, faithfulness, gentleness, and self-control. Every time we see a revelation of the Lord, we see one or more of these nine fruits manifesting through the verse or passage.

When we look at the encounter at the burning bush, we see an example of God's lovingkindness:

> I HAVE SURELY SEEN THE OPPRESSION OF MY PEOPLE WHO ARE IN EGYPT, AND HAVE HEARD THEIR CRY BECAUSE OF THEIR TASKMASTERS, FOR I KNOW THEIR SORROWS. SO I HAVE COME DOWN TO DELIVER THEM OUT OF THE HAND OF THE EGYPTIANS, AND TO BRING THEM UP FROM THAT LAND TO A GOOD AND LARGE LAND, TO A LAND FLOWING WITH MILK AND HONEY.
> ~ EXODUS 3:7–8A

During the wedding at Cana in John 2, we see in verse 10 a picture of God's joy:

> AND HE SAID TO HIM, "EVERY MAN AT THE BEGINNING SETS OUT THE GOOD WINE, AND WHEN THE GUESTS HAVE WELL DRUNK, THEN THE INFERIOR. YOU HAVE KEPT THE GOOD WINE UNTIL NOW!"

Prayer is a chief way of walking in joyful communion with the Lord. It is simply communicating with the Lord. *Lectio divina*, praying the Word of God, is one way of entering into that communication. When we slow down and pray through the Scriptures, we encounter revelations of the Lord we may not have seen before, such as His joy over us.

THE LORD YOUR GOD IN YOUR MIDST,
THE MIGHTY ONE, WILL SAVE;
HE WILL REJOICE OVER YOU WITH GLADNESS,
HE WILL QUIET YOU WITH HIS LOVE,
HE WILL REJOICE OVER YOU WITH SINGING.
~ ZEPHANIAH 3:17

"All that I experienced was shown me in the Holy Scripture. I saw with admiration that there passed nothing within my soul which was not in Jesus Christ and in the Holy Scriptures. I must pass over very many things in silence, because they cannot be expressed. If they were expressed they could not be understood or comprehended."

Autobiography of Madame Guyon

DISCOVERING RENEWED FELLOWSHIP

Just as the Lord speaks in parables through our dreams, Christ would speak in parables to the masses, so they would seek Him out. In the same way, the Lord has given us His Word that holds revelation in every verse. This Word becomes applicable, personal, and full of life only with regular reading.

> IT IS THE GLORY OF GOD TO CONCEAL A MATTER, BUT THE GLORY OF KINGS IS TO SEARCH OUT A MATTER.
> ~ PROVERBS 25:2

When we read His Word, and when we pray His Word back to Him, we are seeking out revelation of Him, and He will reveal Himself to those who seek Him. Like a youth learning the trade of his father, we not only grow in skill, but we also grow in relationship with the Father the more we press in.

Hearing God's voice is not new. People have heard the Lord's voice from the very beginning.

From Genesis 2:7 we know that God gave life to man by breathing into him His very breath of life. He set Adam and Eve before Him in loving relationship and communed with them on a daily basis. The time of day when God came to regularly commune with Adam and Eve was the ninth hour. He called it the evening oblation—that's the cool of the day. He would walk with them during this time of day, when the day's work was finished.

If you remember in Genesis 3:8, man's first contact with God after the fall occurred in the cool of the day—which is the time of the evening oblation.

> AND THEY HEARD THE SOUND OF THE LORD GOD
> WALKING IN THE GARDEN IN THE COOL OF THE DAY,
> AND ADAM AND HIS WIFE HID THEMSELVES FROM THE
> PRESENCE OF THE LORD GOD AMONG THE TREES OF THE
> GARDEN.
> ~ GENESIS 3:8

We learn from the Gospel accounts of the crucifixion that Jesus breathed His last at the evening oblation—at the cool of the day. This was also referred to as the time for the evening sacrifice or the ninth hour.

> NOW IT WAS ABOUT THE SIXTH HOUR, AND THERE WAS
> DARKNESS OVER ALL THE EARTH UNTIL THE NINTH
> HOUR. THEN THE SUN WAS DARKENED, AND THE VEIL
> OF THE TEMPLE WAS TORN IN TWO. AND WHEN JESUS
> HAD CRIED OUT WITH A LOUD VOICE, HE SAID, "FATHER,
> 'INTO YOUR HANDS I COMMIT MY SPIRIT.'" HAVING SAID
> THIS, HE BREATHED HIS LAST.
> ~ LUKE 23:44-46

In Acts we learn that Cornelius, a Gentile and a centurion, was met by an angel at the ninth hour.

> ABOUT THE NINTH HOUR OF THE DAY HE SAW CLEARLY
> IN A VISION AN ANGEL OF GOD COMING IN AND SAYING
> TO HIM, "CORNELIUS!"
>
> AND WHEN HE OBSERVED HIM, HE WAS AFRAID, AND
> SAID, "WHAT IS IT, LORD?"
>
> SO HE SAID TO HIM, "YOUR PRAYERS AND YOUR ALMS
> HAVE COME UP FOR A MEMORIAL BEFORE GOD."
> ~ ACTS 10:3-4

Later it was revealed to Peter in a trance that he should be the one to minister to this Gentile centurion named Cornelius. We see in Acts 10:30 that it was the ninth hour when Peter went to Cornelius to tell him about Jesus. While Peter was speaking to him, the Holy Spirit fell upon Cornelius. It was in the ninth hour that the Gentiles were irrevocably received into the household of faith.

It's interesting to consider that man lost relationship with God at the ninth hour, and man gained relationship with God again at the very same hour. Prior to this event, the Gentiles had little relationship with the Lord. Theirs were not the patriarchs or the covenants, yet they gained the Spirit of Adoption through Christ's work on the Cross. All of this took place at the ninth hour, at the evening oblation, in the cool of the day.

Other amazing things occurred at the time of the evening sacrifice. This was the time when fire fell from Heaven onto the sacrifice at Mount Carmel (1 Kings 18:36–38). It was also the time when Peter and John went to the temple to pray and the lame man who sat at the Beautiful Gate was healed (Acts 3:1–10).

You won't pick up on details such as the occurrences at the ninth hour just by glancing at the Word or by reading through it quickly. You'll pick that up by praying the Word back to God and meditating on those portions He shows to you. Then, when you read the ninth hour, the Holy Spirit will cause you to pause and consider: "Where did I read the ninth hour before?" The Holy Spirit then says, "Remember when you read and prayed it. Look here. Now look here. Now look here." You will soon find that meditation on God's Word and praying through God's Word help you remember what He brought to your attention earlier.

I WILL INSTRUCT YOU AND TEACH YOU
IN THE WAY YOU SHOULD GO;
I WILL GUIDE YOU WITH MY EYE.
~ PSALM 32:8

SHARPER THAN ANY TWO-EDGED SWORD

When the inspired, God-breathed verses of the Bible become our prayer, something powerful occurs. We are praying the anointed words of God. These prayers will release the move of God's Spirit in our lives in a more precise and effective way. It's the Hebrews 4:12 principle:

ALL SCRIPTURE IS GIVEN BY INSPIRATION OF GOD, AND IS PROFITABLE FOR DOCTRINE, FOR REPROOF, FOR CORRECTION, FOR INSTRUCTION IN RIGHTEOUSNESS, THAT THE MAN OF GOD MAY BE COMPLETE, THOROUGHLY EQUIPPED FOR EVERY GOOD WORK.
~2 TIMOTHY 3:16–17

FOR THE WORD OF GOD IS LIVING AND POWERFUL, AND SHARPER THAN ANY TWO-EDGED SWORD, PIERCING EVEN TO THE DIVISION OF SOUL AND SPIRIT, AND OF JOINTS AND MARROW, AND IS A DISCERNER OF THE THOUGHTS AND INTENTS OF THE HEART.

You can pray this verse and say it over and over again, turning it into a prayer to release the work of the Holy Spirit in your life: "The Word of God—Jesus, *Your Word* is sharper and more powerful than any two-edged sword. You are *living*. You pierce like a *two-edged sword*." You pause and consider each word and phrase. This is when you ask the Lord, "What does *this* mean? What does *that* mean?" Then you pray the revelation back to Him: "Lord, You pierce both ways. It doesn't say *one* edge; it says *two* edges. So it cuts both ways. Whatever way Your Word moves, it is going to cut, and You, O Lord, are there. You divide between the things of You and the things that bother me. You divide between the things of You and the things that trouble me. You even divide between the things of this life that seek to lead me away when I know Your Spirit desires to lead me to You."

When you begin praying that way, over and over, you can find yourself spending hours in prayer. There is so much power and effectiveness in praying God's Word.

I encourage you to pause in your reading and ask God questions such as, "Lord, what does that mean? I sense that it is significant, but I don't understand it. Why is this significant? This is Your Word to me. Please show me what it means." Pray your questions about the Word while you are praying the Word of God. He will answer your questions, sometimes in the same time frame of your prayer.

When it says in Philippians 2:12 to "work out your own salvation with fear and trembling," this is one way to walk that out. Position yourself before the awesome presence of the Lord by reading His Word, by praying it back to Him, and by allowing Him to work on your heart and form you into the image of Jesus.

One of the great praying souls of the 19th century, rose at 4 a.m. every day to seek the Lord by his bedside. When he died, his elders found two deep indentations worn into the wood floor where he knelt to pray. "More carefully than ever I hope this year to give two hours before going out every day, to meditate on the Word and prayer. And in this way there shall go out of me heavenward 'rivers of living water' that will bring down refreshing rain-showers."

Andrew Bonar

The Underlying Spiritual Rhythm

Over a short period of time, you'll begin to discover an underlying spiritual rhythm within your prayers. *Lectio divina* helps you discover that rhythm, and as you pray into it, prayer becomes the natural response of searching with an honest heart.

Prayer is our inner beings calling on a holy and almighty God who is greater and higher than His creation. God daily walked and talked with Adam and Eve in the Garden. It was a regular, customary part of their relationship—in other words, part of the rhythm of the day.

In Genesis 3:8–10, we see an example of God practicing the customary rhythm He initiated:

> Unless Your law had been my delight, I would then have perished in my affliction. I will never forget Your precepts, For by them You have given me life. I am Yours, save me; For I have sought Your precepts.
> ~ Psalm 119:92-94

> And they heard the sound of the Lord God walking in the garden in the cool of the day, and Adam and his wife hid themselves from the presence of the Lord God among the trees of the garden. Then the Lord God called to Adam and said to him, "Where are you?" So he said, "I heard Your voice in the garden."

Before the fall, communing with God was a natural part of human existence and part of Adam and Eve's rhythm of life.

From the moment sin disrupted this rhythm and the communion was lost, God worked to restore all of this with us once more.

This underlying spiritual rhythm even predates Adam and Eve, as we see in the first rule, or law, given in Genesis 1:11:

> LET THE EARTH BRING FORTH GRASS, THE
> HERB THAT YIELDS SEED, AND THE FRUIT TREE THAT
> YIELDS FRUIT ACCORDING TO ITS KIND, WHOSE
> SEED IS IN ITSELF, ON THE EARTH.

In the same way, people are to reproduce, not only other people but ideas and faith. First John 4:19 says that we love Him because He first loved us. This follows the guidelines the Lord established for reproduction. It is from His perfect model that there is reproduction of the next generation in like kind. Therefore, He loves and so we also love.

The restless human heart reveals a deep yearning for relationship with the Divine. Although humanity has sought this reconnection with the Lord in often empty, self-delusional ways—including imposed rules, excessive fasting, and self-flagellation—the longing is still evident.

How do we discover this rhythm of God? It becomes self-evident as our wills become His will. Obedience is the key. As we obey His direction and submit to His purposes, our wills then find His will, long for His will, accept His will, follow His will, and soon transform to His will. And in God, everything lies within His rhythm.

I've heard some people say, "Well, what if God's rhythm is not the same as my rhythm?" That's impossible. He is all rhythm. Every rhythm and beat in the universe has its source in Him. He could be one rhythm to me and one rhythm to you at the same moment. He is all sound. He is all color. He is everything.

The cry of our hearts releases God to intervene in the situation of daily life. Job 34:28 declares,

> FOR HE HEARS THE CRY OF THE AFFLICTED.

Psalm 34:15 says,

> THE EYES OF THE LORD ARE ON THE RIGHTEOUS,
> AND HIS EARS ARE OPEN TO THEIR CRY.

Luke 18:1 and 7 echo the same thing:

> THEN HE SPOKE A PARABLE TO THEM, THAT MEN
> ALWAYS OUGHT TO PRAY AND NOT LOSE HEART . . .
> AND SHALL GOD NOT AVENGE HIS OWN ELECT WHO
> CRY OUT DAY AND NIGHT TO HIM, THOUGH HE BEARS
> LONG WITH THEM?

In other words, it seems to us that He takes a long time, while God is waiting for us to get into a place where He can act. We see this in Isaiah 30:18:

> THEREFORE THE LORD WILL WAIT,
> THAT HE MAY BE GRACIOUS TO YOU;
> AND THEREFORE HE WILL BE EXALTED,
> THAT HE MAY HAVE MERCY ON YOU.
> FOR THE LORD IS A GOD OF JUSTICE;
> BLESSED ARE ALL THOSE WHO WAIT FOR HIM.

God is waiting; He is longing to be gracious to you and to pour out His blessing and presence upon you. Blessed are those who wait for Him. When we wait before Him in the posture of praying His Word back to Him, our cups will overflow with the blessings of His mercy and justice.

When we enter into the overflow of His justice and mercy, whatever had previously been considered gain we now count loss compared with the excellence of the knowledge of Christ Jesus our Lord. Whether we have material possessions or not begins to matter less and less the more time we spend with Him. We can say, just as Job did in Job 1:21-22:

> "THE LORD GAVE, AND THE LORD HAS TAKEN AWAY;
> BLESSED BE THE NAME OF THE LORD." IN ALL THIS JOB
> DID NOT SIN NOR CHARGE GOD WITH WRONG.

FRIENDSHIP WITH GOD

Here is a marvelous thing I've noticed about *lectio divina:* the more I pray in this way, the more of myself I am able to offer to the Father. At first I was able to offer only five minutes of myself to Him. I might have spent an hour in prayer, but when I boiled it down, it was really five minutes of concentrated "good stuff." But the more I've done it, the more often it ends up being an hour or more of offering all of me to the Father.

> HOW PRECIOUS IS YOUR LOVINGKINDNESS, O GOD! THEREFORE THE CHILDREN OF MEN PUT THEIR TRUST UNDER THE SHADOW OF YOUR WINGS. THEY ARE ABUNDANTLY SATISFIED WITH THE FULLNESS OF YOUR HOUSE, AND YOU GIVE THEM DRINK FROM THE RIVER OF YOUR PLEASURES.
> ~ PSALM 36:7-8

Imagine that! You end up giving God an hour of your full attention, not just five minutes of good stuff or a brief moment in an hour.

Abraham and Moses were called the friends of God. They developed a close and intimate relationship with Him. This did not happen overnight. It took time. A sign of that close and intimate relationship with God was their constant or continual communication with the Father.

James 2:23 tells us,

> "ABRAHAM BELIEVED GOD, AND IT WAS ACCOUNTED TO HIM FOR RIGHTEOUSNESS." AND HE WAS CALLED THE FRIEND OF GOD.

Abraham was privy to the Lord's counsel. In Genesis 18, the Lord tells Abraham what He's about to do in Sodom and Gomorrah and then allows Abraham to negotiate with Him.

> AND ABRAHAM CAME NEAR AND SAID, "WOULD
> YOU ALSO DESTROY THE RIGHTEOUS WITH THE
> WICKED? SUPPOSE THERE WERE FIFTY RIGHTEOUS
> WITHIN THE CITY; WOULD YOU ALSO DESTROY THE PLACE
> AND NOT SPARE IT FOR THE FIFTY RIGHTEOUS THAT
> WERE IN IT? FAR BE IT FROM YOU TO DO SUCH A THING
> AS THIS, TO SLAY THE RIGHTEOUS WITH THE WICKED,
> SO THAT THE RIGHTEOUS SHOULD BE AS THE WICKED;
> FAR BE IT FROM YOU! SHALL NOT THE JUDGE OF ALL THE
> EARTH DO RIGHT?"
> ~ GENESIS 18:23-25

Instead of striking Abraham down for presumption, the Lord considers each request and question Abraham brings forth. He answers Abraham as if this mere man was truly a part of the council meeting. "So the LORD said, 'If I find in Sodom fifty righteous within the city, then I will spare all the place for their sakes.'" This council continues between the Lord and Abraham, giving us a strong glimpse of what friendship with God looks like on a very personal level.

In Exodus 33:11, we see this friendship with God in Moses' life:

> SO THE LORD SPOKE TO MOSES FACE TO FACE,
> AS A MAN SPEAKS TO HIS FRIEND.

This is a unique position Moses possessed, to be able to converse with the Lord face to face. Instead of presuming upon this position or boasting about it, Moses approached this friendship with great humility and reverence. In Exodus 33, he asks God three questions, but the order in which Moses asks these questions is important to consider. In verse 13, he asks the Lord to "show me now Your way, that I may know You and that I may find grace in Your sight." He then asks for the Lord's presence in verses 15 and 16. Only after Moses has asked to know God's ways and for the Lord's presence does he ask to see God's glory: "And he said, 'Please, show me Your glory'" (Exodus 33:18). The Lord was delighted to reveal Himself to His friend Moses.

The Father sent His only Son so that we would all have the opportunity to enter into this friendship with God.

Jesus called His disciples *friends* and directed them to put into practice the love He had given them. He extends the same invitation to us—to you and me. John 15:13–15 shows this so clearly: "Greater love has no one than this, than to lay down one's life for his friends. You are My friends . . ." So He laid down His life for His friends. For you. For me. Jesus goes on in that chapter to say, "You are My friends if you do whatever I command you. No longer do I call you servants, for a servant does not know what his master is doing; but I have called you friends, for all things that I heard from My Father I have made known to you."

This call of Jesus to His disciples was a call not only to give love but also to trust in God's love. Their obedience to His Word meant trusting in His love. It's because Jesus loves us and laid down His life for us that He looks for a total response of love on our part, a love whose reality is tested by obedience.

So the purpose of this type of prayer is not just to establish relationship with God but also to strengthen an already existing relationship.

Jeremiah 33:3 illustrates this: "Call to Me, and I will answer you, and show you great and mighty things, which you do not know." The result of an ongoing relationship allows us to call on God, and He will show us things we do not know. Abraham J. Heschel, a Jewish theologian from the mid-twentieth century, said, "Prayer does not change God; prayer changes the pray-er."

Therefore, God desires intimacy with us. He desires communion and communication with us. He desires commitment, friendship, love, and affection from us. These aspects of our relationship with God must increase, or our relationship with Him will eventually decrease. You are never in neutral with God. You will not stay the same, and neither will your relationship with God stay the same. If you're not moving forward, you will move backward. Therefore, I tell people, "If you're in the same place you were five years ago, you better think through some things; change needs to happen, and it probably is not God who needs to change." In order for change to happen, it's imperative that we develop effective prayer lives.

Paul writes in 1 Thessalonians 3:12–13:

> AND MAY THE LORD MAKE YOU INCREASE AND ABOUND IN LOVE TO ONE ANOTHER AND TO ALL, JUST AS WE DO TO YOU, SO THAT HE MAY ESTABLISH YOUR HEARTS BLAMELESS IN HOLINESS BEFORE OUR GOD AND FATHER AT THE COMING OF OUR LORD JESUS CHRIST WITH ALL HIS SAINTS.

A process exists within the increase and abounding of love. There is increased holiness, or increased removal of sin in our lives, so that we may walk in a higher calling in Him. It takes a consistent prayer life to ignite the increase, and we have to keep moving forward in prayer to cultivate it.

"Oh brother, pray; in spite of Satan, pray; spend hours in prayer; rather neglect friends than not pray; rather fast, and lose breakfast, dinner, tea, and supper—and sleep too—than not pray. And we must not talk about prayer, we must pray in right earnest. The Lord is near. He comes softly while the virgins slumber. You may almost hear the breathing of the slumberers, and the tread of Him who comes into the camp as David did to Saul's, ere ever we are aware."

Andrew Bonar

THE IMPORTANCE OF UNDERSTANDING THE SCRIPTURES

When Jesus was twelve years old, He went to the temple without the knowledge of His earthly parents. While He was there, He astounded the teachers of the law:

THAT THE GOD OF OUR LORD JESUS CHRIST, THE FATHER OF GLORY, MAY GIVE TO YOU THE SPIRIT OF WISDOM AND REVELATION IN THE KNOWLEDGE OF HIM, THE EYES OF YOUR UNDERSTANDING BEING ENLIGHTENED.
~ EPHESIANS 1:17-18

NOW SO IT WAS THAT AFTER THREE DAYS THEY FOUND HIM IN THE TEMPLE, SITTING IN THE MIDST OF THE TEACHERS, BOTH LISTENING TO THEM AND ASKING THEM QUESTIONS. AND ALL WHO HEARD HIM WERE ASTONISHED AT HIS UNDERSTANDING AND ANSWERS.
~ LUKE 2:46-47

Jesus went on to maturity, and the people marveled not only at His understanding but also at His authority.

AND SO IT WAS, WHEN JESUS HAD ENDED THESE SAYINGS, THAT THE PEOPLE WERE ASTONISHED AT HIS TEACHING, FOR HE TAUGHT THEM AS ONE HAVING AUTHORITY, AND NOT AS THE SCRIBES.
~ MATTHEW 7:28-29

When we pray the Scriptures back to God and ask Him questions about His Word, we gain understanding, like it says in Psalm 119:99: "I have more understanding than all my teachers, for Your testimonies are my meditation." When we meditate on and pray the Word of the Lord, our understanding of Scripture begins to abound. And as our understanding of the Word of God abounds, we increase in authority. Our relationship with the ever-present Author and Finisher of our faith grows deeper as we seek to spend time with Him and to open our hearts before Him during times of reading and praying His Word. And from this depth of relationship, we enter into an authority we didn't have before.

Six-year-old Ludwig was sitting at the table, reading his Bible and praying, when Swedish soldiers stormed through the castle door. Ludwig looked up at the soldiers and then returned to his prayer and reading. The soldiers stopped and stared – then left. They said they could not ransack a place that God watched over.

Count Zinzendorf
written by Janet Benge & Geoff Benge

REMAINING IN HIS EMBRACE

Discipline yourself not to do anything else while you're seeking to be in His embrace. In other words, while you're practicing *lectio divina*, do not watch TV. Do not listen to the radio. Turn off your computers and your gadgets. Do not allow anything to distract you from focusing your full attention on God. Let Him be your full focus. The more often you do this, the more you will discover the gift of an ever-deepening relationship that God continually offers to us through His Son, Jesus Christ.

> THE BELOVED OF THE LORD SHALL DWELL IN SAFETY BY HIM, WHO SHELTERS HIM ALL THE DAY LONG; AND HE SHALL DWELL BETWEEN HIS SHOULDERS.
> ~ DEUTERONOMY 33:12

In John 14:6, Jesus says, "I am the way, the truth, and the life. No one comes to the Father except through Me." We don't develop this relationship with the Father except through Jesus. John 1:14 reads, "The Word became flesh and dwelt among us, and we beheld His glory, the glory as of the only begotten of the Father, full of grace and truth." God sent His living Word to the earth so that we might be transformed, changed, and receive once again what God originally intended for us to have—unending communion with the Father.

When John the Baptist baptized Jesus in Matthew 3:16–17, it heralded a turning point in history:

WHEN HE HAD BEEN BAPTIZED, JESUS CAME UP
IMMEDIATELY FROM THE WATER; AND BEHOLD,
THE HEAVENS WERE OPENED TO HIM, AND HE SAW
THE SPIRIT OF GOD DESCENDING LIKE A DOVE
AND ALIGHTING UPON HIM. AND SUDDENLY A
VOICE CAME FROM HEAVEN, SAYING, 'THIS IS MY
BELOVED SON, IN WHOM I AM WELL PLEASED.'

The Word became flesh and dwelt among us. The Heavens were opened again and the Spirit of God descended. Those present heard the voice of God as He spoke from Heaven.

In Ephesians 2:18, Paul writes, "For through Him we both have access by one Spirit to the Father." We have access to the Father by this same Spirit. This Holy Spirit lives within us, He surrounds us, and He woos us into the Father's embrace.

In Mark 10, a young man runs up to Jesus and asks Him how he could enter eternal life. After Jesus gives the man a brief rundown of the Ten Commandments, the young man insists he's followed all of those laws. Jesus loves this man and hands him a final challenge:

ONE THING YOU LACK: GO YOUR WAY, SELL WHATEVER
YOU HAVE AND GIVE TO THE POOR, AND YOU WILL HAVE
TREASURE IN HEAVEN; AND COME, TAKE UP THE CROSS,
AND FOLLOW ME.
~ MARK 10:21

Jesus addressed the man's one distraction—personal wealth and well-being.

Then Jesus goes on to say:

CHILDREN, HOW HARD IT IS FOR THOSE WHO TRUST IN
RICHES TO ENTER THE KINGDOM OF GOD! IT IS EASIER
FOR A CAMEL TO GO THROUGH THE EYE OF A NEEDLE
THAN FOR A RICH MAN TO ENTER THE KINGDOM OF GOD.
~ MARK 10:24B-25

Jesus is not saying that having riches or money is evil. Many of the women who followed Him were considerably wealthy and provided for Him from their own purses (see Luke 8:3). Lydia, in Acts 16, was a wealthy businesswoman who provided for Paul and encouraged him on his journeys. Job was a very rich man, and after his time of testing, his wealth was restored to him in double portion. Boaz, who married Ruth, was a very well-to-do farmer. Having riches is not bad, but *trusting* in riches or money can be a major distraction in the life of anyone sincere about following Him. We must be willing to pick up the Cross and follow Jesus. Money was this young man's distraction.

What is it that distracts you or pulls you away from the Lord's embrace? It could be a person, a gadget, or a hobby. How can you remove this distraction from your life? Have you considered asking the Holy Spirit for help? He is the Helper and will supernaturally remove distractions if you ask Him to.

TAKE A MOMENT TO SEEK THE LORD ABOUT THE DISTRACTIONS THAT ARE HINDERING YOUR WALK WITH HIM.

O my Father, my God, deliver me, I beseech you, from all violent passions: I know how greatly obstructive these are of both the knowledge and the love of You. Oh, let none of them find a way into my heart, but let me ever possess my soul in meekness. O my God, I desire to fear them more than death; let me not serve these cruel tyrants, but do You reign in my breast; let me be ever Your servant, and love You with all my heart.

John Wesley

THE RHYTHM OF SPIRITUAL OSCILLATION

This brings us to the rhythm of spiritual oscillation. In our lives, we daily oscillate between the poles of hurried activity and quiet receptivity, between practice and doing, between contemplation and being still. At first, the oscillation appears to be circular. This is because we often become insensitive to spiritual beckoning or the increase or decrease of spiritual intensity surrounding us. Therefore, we perceive little evidence of upward progress in our walk with the Lord. To many of us, it may even seem as if we're constantly chasing ourselves instead of arriving at the shores of a spiritual contentment.

> I WILL MEDITATE ON
> YOUR PRECEPTS,
> AND CONTEMPLATE
> YOUR WAYS.
> I WILL DELIGHT MYSELF
> IN YOUR STATUTES;
> I WILL NOT FORGET YOUR
> WORD.
> ~ PSALM 119:15-16

We keep doing the same devotional reading of the Word, and our minds wander. Consequently, we fail to apply what we have read to our lives, and we keep making the same mistakes we made in the past. If we give this repetitive cycle a cursory observation, it simply keeps repeating itself over and over in our lives. But with the added dimensions of time and rumination, we end those cycles, and the spiritual activity now begins to look like a helix that spirals upward.

Science tells us that the helix is the best conductor of energy there is, and the DNA strand is the most efficient and effective transferor of energy in the helix family. The angle of the strand and the turn of the strand are what make it the most efficient conductor and transferor of electricity. That's why science is now trying to make computer chips based on nanotechnology that would use DNA as the transfer mechanism. While I pray they never succeed, they are nonetheless attempting to do this. Science is trying to capitalize on this reality.

Over months and years of time spent in consistent prayer, we sometimes think nothing is changing in our lives and that we are simply repeating the same prayers over and over again. But that isn't true. When we picture the helix, we can see that we are actually working our way up to the Father, and despite the seemingly repetitive nature of our prayers, we are uttering prayers at a higher spiritual plane than we were a year ago. Without knowing it, we have prayed our way into a closer relationship with Him. And if we mapped that prayer journey out, it would look much less like a circle and more like the progression of a spiritual helix. Building a personal history of prayer builds your personal spiritual foundation.

As we build this foundational history of prayer with God, we are building momentum as well. *Lectio divina*, as a mode of prayer, is a fruitful way to increase spiritual momentum and grow in the art of hearing God.

God has designed our minds to actually help us by alerting us to notice the things that are important to us. This system, called the reticular activating system (RAS), is a part of our brains that helps us recall something we habitually visit or want to notice, either in study or in action. If we continually position ourselves before the Word of God and before the Lord in prayer, the RAS will begin to build a matrix of memory surrounding those times of prayer. When we position ourselves to pray, we may not consciously recall the details of the last time we sat down to pray, but our brains will add to the memory of the last experience. That is an important portion of what Paul called "being renewed in the spirit of your mind." It is also how the spiritual helix is built. Each time of prayer becomes spiritually higher than the last time, whether it feels that way or not. Because the soul cannot be trusted to recognize increasing spiritual maturity; spirit-to-Spirit movement will always be resisted by the soul, and the soul is an inconsistent measuring stick. Just look at the different emotions you experience each day. No matter what the soul (our emotions) might tell us, the pathway of the spiritual helix rises each time we pray. We are drawing ever closer to the Father.

This is the Lord's work from beginning to end. He is the One who designed the RAS into our spiritual makeup. He is the One who woos us into time away with Him. He is the One who allows our simple obedience to be part of what builds strong relationship with Him.

> BRETHREN, I DO NOT COUNT MYSELF TO HAVE
> APPREHENDED; BUT ONE THING I DO, FORGETTING THOSE
> THINGS WHICH ARE BEHIND AND REACHING FORWARD
> TO THOSE THINGS WHICH ARE AHEAD, I PRESS TOWARD
> THE GOAL FOR THE PRIZE OF THE UPWARD CALL OF GOD
> IN CHRIST JESUS.
> ~ PHILIPPIANS 3:13-14

I pray because I can't help myself.
I pray because I'm helpless.
I pray because the need flows out of me all the time—
waking and sleeping.
It doesn't change God—it changes me.

C.S. Lewis

Four Stages of *Lectio Divina*

The four stages of *lectio divina* are commonly referred to by their Latin names: *lectio, meditatio, oratio* and *contemplatio*.

MAN SHALL NOT LIVE BY BREAD ALONE, BUT BY EVERY WORD THAT PROCEEDS FROM THE MOUTH OF GOD.
~ MATTHEW 4:4

Lectio–**Reading/listening:** This is where you slowly read through the selected portion of Scripture, all the while listening to what the Lord speaks to you from His Word. He may not speak directly but highlight a particular word or phrase.

Meditatio–**Meditation:** This is the stage where you meditate and ruminate on the particular word or phrase the Lord highlighted to you while reading His Word.

Oratio–**Prayer:** You then pray the Scriptures back to God, focusing on the portion that stood out to you the most, repeating them as the Spirit moves you to do so.

Contemplatio–**Contemplation and rumination:** In silence and stillness before the Lord, utter thankfulness and praise in your heart. Apply the chosen Scriptures to your life, place your name into the verse, then simply rest in the Lord's presence and allow Him to change you. The Word of God is truly a living Word of God, and as it is a spiritually living and breathing life force, you cannot read it without being changed—life begets life. The change may not be recognizable or instantaneous, but pray in this fashion, and over time change will inevitably come. Strangely enough, this change will often be obvious to others before it is evident to you.

THE NINE STEPS

There are nine steps I recommend for preparing the body, soul, and spirit for *lectio divina* and then entering into a time of prayer. I will explain these steps in further detail in the subsequent chapters, but here they are in summary:

Step 1 - Choose to discipline yourself to pray.
Step 2 - Prepare the body and soul.
Step 3 - Recognize God wants to commune with you.
Step 4 - Listen deeply to God's truth for your life.
Step 5 - Read *and* listen while reading.
Step 6 - Pray with intensity.
Step 7 - Contemplate and apply.
Step 8 - Abide in God.
Step 9 - Journal to seal the moment.

Choose to exercise the desire, discipline, and delight of this form of prayer.

BUT I DISCIPLINE MY BODY AND BRING IT INTO SUBJECTION, LEST, WHEN I HAVE PREACHED TO OTHERS, I MYSELF SHOULD BECOME DISQUALIFIED.
~ I CORINTHIANS 9:27

You can do all the steps or just one of them, but you must choose to start, and you must choose to be consistent in this discipline. Your choice will determine the depth of His response. This is where transformation begins, but choosing can only come with desire. In fact, it is often hard to tell which comes first—discipline or desire—but we do know that delight does not come before discipline or before desire. So the progression is that desire leads to discipline, and discipline leads to delight. *Lectio divina* is the practice that facilitates the experience of spiritual delight, and it is in the experience of delight that time becomes less important as we touch the edge of eternity.

Lectio divina is an inward discipline. It is one of three types of spiritual disciplines: inward, outward, and integral. Inward impacts our inner relationship with God; outward impacts our relationships with others, and integral impacts our interactions with the world.

Choosing *lectio divina* is much like choosing a "handle" that helps us grasp God better, but it requires a response from us. We must apply what we hear in His living Word. When we respond in this manner, we are promised that we will hear more. Jesus explained to His disciples about hearing and responding when He told them why He spoke in parables. The scribes referred to in the Old Testament once heard from God, but they had strayed far from Him, and as a result, God had taken away their ability to hear Him. Jesus wanted His disciples not only to hear but to hear Him *more*. Parables were a way for His disciples to hear even though the scribes, who once heard, could no longer hear at all.

AND THE DISCIPLES CAME AND SAID TO HIM, "WHY DO YOU SPEAK TO THEM IN PARABLES?" HE ANSWERED AND SAID TO THEM, "BECAUSE IT HAS BEEN GIVEN TO YOU TO KNOW THE MYSTERIES OF THE KINGDOM OF HEAVEN . . . FOR WHOEVER HAS, TO HIM MORE WILL BE GIVEN, AND HE WILL HAVE ABUNDANCE; BUT WHOEVER DOES NOT HAVE, EVEN WHAT HE HAS WILL BE TAKEN AWAY FROM HIM."
~ MATTHEW 13:10-12

The scribes and Pharisees had lost their desire, their self-discipline, and consequently they would no longer experience the delight of the intimacy it takes to hear. They had become so jaded to God's presence that they no longer could recognize when He was near—evidenced by the Son of God standing in their midst and them not knowing it.

Lectio divina is one way to guarantee you'll keep hearing from God and can legitimately expect to hear and know more tomorrow than today.

The discipline of practice is vital to rising up the helix of spiritual prayer. Imagine you were visited by an angel who told you that you had a gift to play the piano, but you would have to practice and hone that skill. The blessing of having the gift would be a great aid in helping you be consistent in your practice, because you knew it would lead to an expression that would bring you and others pleasure and joy.

In the same manner, you have a word from God. He wants you to know Him, to hear from Him, and to have a relationship with Him. In so doing, you will become a change agent, and anyone who comes near you will be changed as he or she encounters the increased measure of the Holy Spirit dwelling within you. To the degree you are transformed through the practice of *lectio divina* and other spiritual practices, you will change those you meet.

> DISCIPLINE YOURSELF FOR THE PURPOSE OF GODLINESS.
> ~1 TIMOTHY 4:7 (NASB)

I recognize that discipline alone will not make a person holy. Scripture is clear that holiness is a result of being close to the One who is holy. However, John, in recording the words of Jesus, does say that the Word sanctifies those who have a life in it.

> SANCTIFY THEM BY YOUR TRUTH. YOUR WORD IS TRUTH.
> ~JOHN 17:17

Therefore, the discipline of time spent reading the Word of God will change one's life and family, as truth from the Word removes the lies of the world.

PREPARING THE BODY AND SOUL

IN THE MULTITUDE OF MY
ANXIETIES WITHIN ME, YOUR
COMFORTS DELIGHT MY SOUL.
~ PSALM 94:19

Over the years when I have taught about prayer, a number of individuals have asked me how to deal with various physical issues that distract or hinder their attempts to pray. Talking with someone at the end of a class one evening, I said, "Sometimes our body is our enemy, and broadly speaking, we have to tell our body what to do. Sometimes we have to calmly say to our bodies, 'Peace, be still.' And sometimes that requires speaking to one part of your body at a time. For example, you can speak to the big toe and say, 'Big toe, on my left foot, stop moving. Toe next to it, be still; stop moving. Foot, be still; stop moving. Relax.'" Admittedly, this may seem strange to some, but if you are like me, there are times when one part of my body wants to fidget or move in some manner, and this can be distracting.

In Scripture the term "peace, be still" is most often associated with Jesus speaking to the storm on the Sea of Galilee. Historians tell us Jesus most likely spoke Hebrew, not Greek, so the word He used for "peace" would have been *shalom*. The root of *shalom* means more than calm or tranquility: it also means the removal of anarchy or stress, which results in calm and tranquility. Thus Jesus, by using the word *shalom*, commanded the anarchy and stress inherent in the storm to be removed, and the result was that peace and tranquility came. As you know, the winds and waves ceased, and the storm stopped.

I have often had to speak to my body and mind in that way. I have to calmly declare *shalom* and command anarchy and stress to leave my thoughts and physical system.

At times, I have even had to start with one toe at a time and work my way up my body. I find that if my toe is not tapping, my finger is tapping or my knees are moving. My knees move almost constantly. They don't move because I'm nervous; my body is just constantly moving. So I often have to tell my body to stop moving or, "*Shalom.*"

In 2 Chronicles 7:14 we read, "If My people who are called by My name will humble themselves . . ." It is humbling to recognize that your body is not willing to fully cooperate with your spiritual quest, and it takes real effort to get your body into a physical position of readiness to pray. I don't necessarily mean kneeling or lying prostrate, but I do mean coming to a place of internal and external stillness. You still yourself. You place yourself in a relaxed, comfortable position. You quiet your mind and your body.

Some of you may be like I am. My life is so full, time is always spoken for, demands are always present, and it seems that I'd go to sleep if I relaxed. That may occasionally happen to you. But if you keep disciplining yourself, and if you keep stilling yourself before the Lord, eventually that will not be a problem. Your body will begin to long for the delight that lies ahead. I used to fall asleep as soon as I relaxed, but I don't have that problem now. Now I find my body is ready to relax and welcomes the quieting of my spirit. That is how we can prepare the body for a time of prayer. A byproduct of this practice is that we are actually training our spirits to lead, as well as training our souls to submit to the leading of the Holy Spirit.

How do we prepare the soul? One must approach God with a spirit of humility and repentance. These heart attitudes always open us to God's blessings and His presence. Sometimes we have to change our environment to make the interchange of soul rule to spirit rule. Solitude, getting away from outside distractions, often plays a significant role in this process.

Dallas Willard, in his book *The Spirit of the Disciplines: Understanding How God Changes Lives*, writes, "Solitude can be transforming, however, like all of the disciplines of the spirit, it carries its risks. In solitude, we confront our own soul with its obscure forces and conflicts that escape our attention when we're interacting with others." In other words, only when we're alone does the soul pounce on us. When we're interacting with others, the interaction keeps us from recognizing what our souls are doing.

He adds, "We can only survive solitude if we cling to Christ in the moment. What we find when we cling to Him in the place of solitude is that we're enabled to return to society a free person." For more on this subject, I recommend Mr. Willard's book.

Jesus spent time in profound solitude and silence, setting an example for us. After He was baptized, He was led by the Holy Spirit into the solitude of the wilderness where He was tempted by the devil. He was there in the wilderness for forty days. I might note that it was His time in the wilderness that allowed Jesus to begin His ministry in the "power of the Spirit"(Luke 4:14).

Even while He ministered through Galilee, Judea, and the surrounding regions, He often took time to be alone and pray. There was one particular evening He spent in solitude, praying to the Father all night long. The next morning He began to select the twelve men who were to be His disciples. At another time, He sent the crowds away and put His disciples on a boat, telling them to meet Him later on the other side of the lake. He prayed from sundown until the fourth watch of the night—or between 3:00 a.m. and 6:00 a.m., the final watch before sunrise.

On the night before He was crucified, Jesus prayed alone in the Garden of Gethsemane. After asking His friends to pray with Him, He walked over to a separate spot to focus on prayer. But He ended up praying alone because His disciples fell asleep. Later, Jesus said the reason they fell asleep was that their spirits were willing to pray, but their flesh, their physical bodies, was weak. Meanwhile, the body of Jesus—knowing what He was about to face in bearing the wrath of God on the Cross—began to react and respond by sweating drops of blood.

Jesus is our Great Forerunner and ever lives to intercede for us. We may never face anguish even close to what He experienced in that hour of solitude, but we can trust that He is acquainted with our sufferings. "For we do not have a High Priest who cannot sympathize with our weaknesses, but was in all points tempted as we are, yet without sin" (Hebrews 4:15).

Silence and solitude aren't always difficult and painful. In Psalm 131:2 we find a picture of someone content in silence and solitude:

> SURELY I HAVE CALMED AND QUIETED MY SOUL,
> LIKE A WEANED CHILD WITH HIS MOTHER;
> LIKE A WEANED CHILD IS MY SOUL WITHIN ME.

Have you ever watched an infant who just finished eating? If the child doesn't fall right to sleep, he or she rests silently and contentedly against the mother, listening to her heartbeat. If you cultivate childlikeness as you practice this type of silence, you will reap peace.

Ask the Holy Spirit to come and fill you with His peace. Remember, peace/*shalom* is the fertile potting soil for revelation and prayer. Be aware that your body and soul will fight against the peace the Holy Spirit wants to bring, because your body and soul want to remain in control. They don't want your spirit to control, but don't allow this to discourage you. While it is normal, it can be conquered.

You may find that your mind tends to wander at first. Don't let that discourage you either. It's to be expected because your mind is not used to being still and focused. Simply be thankful for every moment you give God, whether those moments are few or many. In the beginning, you may find that keeping a notepad close by helps. Why? Because after you have written down the thought that distracts you from prayer, your mind is free, and you will find it easier to focus on what the Holy Spirit is placing on your heart. You will not need the notepad for long as your ability to focus increases.

As you grow in this prayer practice, your ability to center on things of the Spirit will strengthen. Some Christians focus on their breathing as a way to slow down the mind. They take in deep breaths through the nose and let them out through the mouth, all the while inviting the presence of the Holy Spirit to fill them in their times of prayer. They do this until their entire bodies are relaxed, stress leaves, and peace enters them.

Consider calmly reciting a favorite song, verse, or poem. There may be a song you know that quotes Scripture, and as you revisit this song in your mind, you calm and can quiet the three areas of your soul: mind, will, and emotions.

When you align your will to God's, purposely focusing yourself to seek Him, you give His Holy Spirit the opportunity to lead. If you're used to constantly moving, working, and doing things, this may be a struggle the first few times. Don't let the struggle discourage you, but constantly and consciously choose the Lord. Making this decision to spend time with the Lord will gradually lessen the struggle.

You may be going through a time of emotional upheaval, during which it's difficult to focus on anything besides the pain you feel. This was true even with Jesus before His crucifixion. His soul was actively forcing Him to think about His coming pain, but His prayer of "not My will but Yours be done" conquered that initial distraction. What better time is there to connect with the Lord than during those seasons of poignant pain? In drawing close to the Father during His time of hardship, Jesus was able to put the Father's desire above His pain. You, too, may have painful times, but in the moment of heartache, as you continually open up to the Lord and plainly tell Him how much it hurts and how it strips you of your ability to focus on Him, the more He will bring you to a place where you can focus on Him above the pain of the situation. Many psalms follow this pattern, and Psalm 69 is a classic illustration of this:

> SAVE ME, O GOD,
> FOR THE WATERS HAVE COME UP TO MY NECK.
> I SINK IN THE MIRY DEPTHS,
> WHERE THERE IS NO FOOTHOLD.
> I HAVE COME INTO THE DEEP WATERS;
> THE FLOODS ENGULF ME.
> I AM WORN OUT CALLING FOR HELP;
> MY THROAT IS PARCHED. (NIV)

MY EYES FAIL,
LOOKING FOR MY GOD.
~ PSALM 69:1–3

I WILL PRAISE GOD'S NAME IN SONG
AND GLORIFY HIM WITH THANKSGIVING.
~ PSALM 69:30

As he poured out his heart before the Lord, David's emotions, although valid given his situation, took a back seat to praise by the end of the psalm. So even in the middle of heartache and profound sorrow, we can connect with the heart of God through devotional and contemplative prayer. The moment we feel the deep healing His presence brings us, we can run with eager and open arms to the Father.

We can submit our entire souls to the Holy Spirit's leading, and He will help us to become still before Him.

BE STILL, AND KNOW THAT I AM GOD.
~ PSALM 46:10

RECOGNIZE GOD WANTS TO COMMUNE WITH YOU

Jesus spoke one of the most deeply significant passages concerning how passionate God is about communing with us. He told the disciples that the very Spirit of God will speak to us, tell us, bring the things of God to us, teach us, and declare to us everything we need to know about the ways of God.

God's primary means for giving us guidance is through the Bible. The Bible is the "rule book" that builds our faith and the design for living our lives. If we know and understand the Scriptures, we will be well on our way to hearing what God might want to communicate with us. He will never guide His people contrary to the clear principles of His written Word.

> I STILL HAVE MANY THINGS TO SAY TO YOU, BUT YOU CANNOT BEAR THEM NOW. HOWEVER, WHEN HE, THE SPIRIT OF TRUTH, HAS COME, HE WILL GUIDE YOU INTO ALL TRUTH; FOR HE WILL NOT SPEAK ON HIS OWN AUTHORITY, BUT WHATEVER HE HEARS HE WILL SPEAK; AND HE WILL TELL YOU THINGS TO COME. HE WILL GLORIFY ME, FOR HE WILL TAKE OF WHAT IS MINE AND DECLARE IT TO YOU. ALL THINGS THAT THE FATHER HAS ARE MINE. THEREFORE I SAID THAT HE WILL TAKE OF MINE AND DECLARE IT TO YOU.
> - JOHN 16:12-15

Increased communion with God comes from a knowledge of God Himself. In *lectio divina*, we discover what pleases and displeases Him. There is no substitute for walking with God, spending time with Him, and talking to Him daily. As you do these things, He will commune with you, and you will come to know what He desires.

THE HUMBLE HE GUIDES IN JUSTICE,
AND THE HUMBLE HE TEACHES HIS WAY.
~PSALM 25:9

I WILL INSTRUCT YOU AND TEACH YOU
IN THE WAY YOU SHOULD GO;
I WILL GUIDE YOU WITH MY EYE.
~PSALM 32:8

This level of relationship with God does not happen overnight. It develops over a period of time; it is not instantaneous. Through practice, your senses become sharpened so that you know good from evil.

You need to have knowledge of the Scriptures and a personal knowledge of God, as well as the awareness that you are living each day in tune with Him, expecting Him to commune with you.

In his book *Knowing God,* J. I. Packer says, "God has spoken to man, and the Bible is His Word, given to us to make us wise unto salvation." Communing with God through *lectio divina* is a great aid in growing in wisdom and purity of heart. Paul wrote that all Scripture is God breathed and useful for teaching and training us—which is communing with us.

God walked and talked with Adam and Eve in the Garden—until the fall. Jesus, the last Adam, gave His life so that man could be reconciled with the Father. It is through this reconciliation that communion with God was restored. God so longed to commune with us that He sent His Son to restore our relationship with Him. He really wants to help us achieve the purpose for which we were created.

TRUST IN THE LORD WITH ALL YOUR HEART,
AND LEAN NOT ON YOUR OWN UNDERSTANDING;
IN ALL YOUR WAYS ACKNOWLEDGE HIM,
AND HE SHALL DIRECT YOUR PATHS.
~PROVERBS 3:5-6

Deep Listening: Hearing with the Ears of the Heart

This may sound oxymoronic, but to listen effectively you must learn to love the spiritual potency of silence. You must love this as much as you would enjoy a conversation with someone. After time spent practicing the discipline of silence and solitude, you long to hear silence. Why? Because when our souls are quiet, the whisper of God is heard. The greatest noise that hinders our hearing is not so much the sound of our voices; it is the noise in our minds.

> He who has an ear, let him hear what the Spirit says to the churches. To him who overcomes I will give to eat from the tree of life, which is in the midst of the Paradise of God.
>
> ~ Revelation 2:7

In the beginning of spiritual practices, we often have to remove the exterior noises before we can quiet our interior lives. Therefore, we find that we hear the voice of the Lord more consistently in a place of silence. One word from God is worth a year of man's conversations—it could even be worth a decade or a lifetime of conversations.

There was a time when I had so many demands on my life that I told my wife, "Honey, I have to get away. I need silence. I need a year of it. I'm aching for silence. I'm aching for it!" I have found that when you rest your body and your soul in silence and attune your ear to His still, small voice, you'll hear Him, just like Elijah did on Mount Horeb in 1 Kings 19:12–13:

AND AFTER THE EARTHQUAKE A FIRE, BUT THE LORD WAS NOT IN THE FIRE; AND AFTER THE FIRE A STILL SMALL VOICE.

SO IT WAS, WHEN ELIJAH HEARD IT, THAT HE WRAPPED HIS FACE IN HIS MANTLE AND WENT OUT AND STOOD IN THE ENTRANCE OF THE CAVE. SUDDENLY A VOICE CAME TO HIM, AND SAID, "WHAT ARE YOU DOING HERE, ELIJAH?"

As you practice the discipline of silence, pay heed to your enhanced and increased ability to listen deeply. In order to listen deeply, you must hear with the ears of your heart. Soften your heart to receive every word the Lord will speak.

The more the water of His Word falls upon a receptive heart, the softer that heart will be. This will sensitize you to the presence of the Holy Spirit and to the quiet sense of His lifting when you're acting outside His will. This level of perception will increase your potential to receive revelation, enlightenment, instruction, and clarification.

When you pay heed to His Word, it brings light to you. "The entrance of Your word gives light;" Psalm 119:130 says, and God wants us to be "enlightened with the light of life" (Job 33:30).

Silence creates an atmosphere where the whisper of God's voice can bring light into our lives.

It was a habit of George Fox to wait in silence for the movement of the Holy Spirit and then begin to pray, causing whole congregations to be shaken and humbled under the hand of God Almighty. "As he prayed the power of God came down in such a marvelous manner the very building seemed to rock."

George Fox

READ *AND* LISTEN WHILE READING

The first part of *lectio divina* is the art of reading while listening to the Lord. You have prepared your body, you have prepared your soul, and now it's time to start reading. Turn to your chosen text, and while reading place your name in the verse when applicable. This is very important to your growth and development in the Lord.

BETTER IS A DRY MORSEL WITH QUIETNESS, THAN A HOUSE FULL OF FEASTING WITH STRIFE. ~ PROVERBS 17:1

I'm going to use Proverbs 17:1 to demonstrate how to insert your name as you read: "Better, John Paul, is a dry morsel that you would receive with quietness than a house full of feasting with strife. John Paul, it is better to have quietness than to have strife. It's better to have a dry morsel with quietness than a house full of feasting with strife."

After praying in this manner, I inquire of the Lord: "Lord, I need that quietness within me. I need it. Even if it's a morsel of quietness, I need it in me. My house isn't full of strife, but it is full of activity. I need that quietness. Still me before You. Speak to me. Help me. Enter me. Increase the measure of Your presence within me. I'm starving for even a morsel of You in quietness. My mind is active. I keep going after things. Help me to wait quietly before You. I don't want strife in my mind, and I don't want strife in my house. I don't want activity to overwhelm my hunger for You. I don't want busyness to distract me, where time rushes by and I forget to seek You. Help me!"

That is what the practice of *lectio divina* might look and sound like in your life. It is reading the Word, applying it to your life, and praying its application into your life. Just pray it. This isn't meant to be fancy, poetic words. It is meant to be you and the Word of God applied to you. It is through the personality God gave you. It is your gift, and it comes from where you are in life.

It may take you five minutes. It may take you five hours. Savor every moment spent in the Lord's presence!

Intensive Prayer

Speaking to God is like having a loving two-way conversation between intimate friends. Intensive prayer is a dialogue with God in which we actually cease from *doing* and transition to *being* in Him. Here in this intimate setting, we become so still we can hear His voice and rest in His presence. For example,

Search me, O God,
and know my heart;
Try me, and know
my anxieties;
And see if there is
any wicked way in me,
And lead me in the
way everlasting.
~ Psalm 139:23-24

look at Mary and Martha in Luke 10. One was *doing* and was busy about her work, while the other was *being* and simply sitting at the feet of Jesus.

The apostle John was known as one who rested his head on Jesus' breast. He was the one Jesus loved (John 13:23). As he reclined there, he ceased from doing and rested in the Lord's presence. Even though he began his walk with Jesus as a "son of thunder" (see Mark 3:17), meaning a very vocal, opinionated, and crude man, John was changed to the point that he sought nothing more than to be close to the Lord. Bible historians tell us that through the latter part of his life John was known as the Apostle of Love.

This closeness stilled John until he could see the Lord. He came to the point where he learned, wrote, and lived, "God is love" (1 John 4:16). The revelation that changed John's life came from a place of *being* before the Lord.

Intensive prayer is offering to Him the deepest parts of us—even the hidden, ugly fragments we are afraid to bring into the light, such as our sin or our deepest, shameful, pain-filled experiences no one else knows about—even the ones we are too embarrassed to confess to God. When we surrender our failures, our sin, and our pain, God can deliver us, He can heal us, and He will make us whole. The truth is . . . He already knows everything about us. He is simply waiting for us to tell Him.

If we don't surrender all those parts of ourselves—if we conceal them—they will never stop bothering us. Even if we carefully hide these things in the deepest parts of us so that people can't see them, our spirits know the pain, regret, sin, and failures are still there. Only when these dark areas are willingly brought into the open before God do they disappear, and He heals those painful and ugly places inside us. God then takes it even further. He takes those things to the point where our spirits, souls, and bodies can no longer access them.

Some of us don't feel worthy to let go of pain and regret. It is as if the memory we have of the problem is part of our punishment. We feel so unworthy, like we deserve the pain, but that's our line of thinking—our idea, not God's. As David said, God's idea is that when our spirits make a diligent search, they can't find what we just gave to God and what He healed us of.

We offer up to Him, in faith, the pain that we have, the failures, and the disappointments. We allow Him to take these things and heal them. We tell Him about them. We discuss them with Him. Then we give them to Him and leave them there.

There are times when we are contradictory within ourselves. Sometimes we tell ourselves, "God knows everything," and in the very next moment we say, "But I can't tell God this." The truth is that in God's omniscience, He already knows everything, so we might as well tell Him. Telling Him is not going to make God say, "Oh, man, I wish you hadn't told Me that." That is not what we're going to hear from God. What we're going to hear from God is, "Finally, you're going to let go of this thing so I can hide it in the deepest sea. Even your spirit can't find it again, and now I can get on with helping you reach your purpose."

He will again have compassion on us,
And will subdue our iniquities.
You will cast all our sins
Into the depths of the sea.

~ Micah 7:19

In the place of intensive prayer, when we open our hearts wide and offer our whole selves to the Father, we can sometimes feel the healing process of letting go happen. And sometimes, as we offer ourselves to Him, His love spills onto us like a holy anesthetic as He removes all the pain and sin, and we are left with an incredible lightness of heart. Few things are as heavy as an old memory of an old sin we have not been able to forget. That's why we feel so much power and relief when we finally let it go.

CONTEMPLATION

One morning, I sat in the armchair in my bedroom and opened my Bible to practice *lectio divina*. It was early enough that the first hints of dawn hadn't yet hit the sky. As I prayed through the Scriptures, the Lord met me in a powerful way. I dove into the rivers of His pleasures, as spoken of in Psalm 36:8:

> AND I WILL
> DELIGHT
> MYSELF IN YOUR
> COMMANDMENTS,
> WHICH I LOVE.
> ~ PSALM 119:47

YOU GIVE THEM DRINK FROM THE RIVER OF YOUR PLEASURES.

I started praying when it was dark, and when I finished it was still dark. I thought only ten minutes had gone by. I had no idea that eleven *hours* had gone by. I did not remember the sun coming up or the sun going down. The windows were open, so I would have been able to see sunlight and the outside. I was so overwhelmed by the Lord's presence that I lost track of time. It was as if I entered God's eternal presence and time was no longer a thought.

You may be thinking, *I can't do that. If I lost track of time in that way, my kids would never get to school!*

Don't you think God knows that? God does know it! He knows us and knows our circumstances, and He knows our children have needs. If He calls us to come away with Him into prayer for an extended period of time, He will call us when circumstances allow that level of intimacy. Sometimes He draws us away like that to show us that everything depends on Him, not on us.

The experience of praying continuously for eleven hours happened to me only one time, but I long for it every day, and I will never forget getting caught up in the Lord's eternal presence like that! You never do forget those moments. You have no hunger and no need for anything, just God.

Those moments mark you. And it happened to me through the practice of *lectio divina*, praying the Word of God. The Word became alive to me and in me that morning. It cascaded through me. It was as if the words coming out of my mouth were coming out of my bone marrow.

So read and pray. Don't seek information while you're praying; instead, allow God to use Scripture to teach you. Allow God to speak to you, and allow yourself to listen to Him. Taking deep breaths will keep you from talking so God can say something.

Allow moments of stillness to occur without feeling guilty. It doesn't take special knowledge, and it doesn't take special expertise. It is just you and Him. He doesn't care if you are skilled in how you do it. He cares about you.

Every day we must release ourselves from our self-imposed limitations and into His purpose. Just because we did it one way yesterday does not mean that we are capable of doing it the same way today. As Exodus 32:29 says, "Consecrate yourselves today to the Lord, that He may bestow on you a blessing this day."

Part of *lectio divina* is the practice of contemplation. This means that you meditate at length, reflect on, and ruminate on what you have read. You think—yet at the same time you still your inner voice. This is not rapid thinking but intentional thinking, ruminating, or what I call *slow thinking*. The idea of ruminating can invoke the image of a cow chewing its cud: constantly turning over and savoring different aspects of a word or phrase in a slow, methodical, rhythmic manner.

Contemplation is pondering God's truth in your heart. Luke 2:19 says that Mary, the mother of Jesus, "kept all these things and pondered *them* in her heart." She contemplated what people said to her about her Son, Jesus. Memorization of His Word will aid your endeavor to practice this type of prayer, and contemplation helps you ponder it. "Your Word I have hidden in my heart, that I might not sin against You" (Psalm 119:11).

Once you have chosen a Bible verse, gently repeat that verse over and over to yourself until the words begin to lose their savor. It could take a minute or an hour. When that happens, go on to the next verse.

Perhaps you're not just reading one verse; you are reading and contemplating an entire passage. Gently repeat the Bible verses or passage to yourself. Let's look at Psalm 23 as an example. Allow the words to interact with your thoughts: "The Lord is my Shepherd; I shall not want…" Allow the words to interact with your hopes, your memories, your desires, and your dreams: "Lord, how I long to lie down in the peace of Your green pastures and rest in peace beside still waters! I desire that You would restore my soul. I am so confused. Father, this last season I went through pain and heartache, and I need my soul to be restored. I thank You that You lead me in paths of righteousness for Your name's sake. Please help me to serve You well and not to stray from Your righteousness."

By doing this, you allow God's Word to change you. Inevitably during this process, God's truths touch and affect you. The longer you practice *lectio divina*, the deeper it touches you until it affects even the deepest level of who you are. That usually won't take place the first few times you do it. You may think it does because you have been touched at a deeper level than you have been touched before. However, God will take you to *many* deeper levels, and the journey takes practice and consistency.

Sometimes a single word or one phrase will fill your whole prayer time. You may go on to another text or return several times to the same text. Like I said, for more than a month, I couldn't stop reading Proverbs 8.

YOUR WORD IS VERY PURE;
THEREFORE YOUR SERVANT LOVES IT.
~PSALM 119:140

God's Word is very pure. It is perfect. It doesn't matter how many days you spend on one verse or passage; what matters is that you are connecting with the Father.

Contemplation is simply resting in His presence. It's putting aside our thoughts, listening for His thoughts, and enjoying His silence, not expecting lightning or visitations from angels but rejoicing in anything God chooses to do in whatever manner He chooses to do it.

SO IT WAS, WHEN THE ANGELS HAD GONE AWAY FROM THEM INTO HEAVEN, THAT THE SHEPHERDS SAID TO ONE ANOTHER, "LET US NOW GO TO BETHLEHEM AND SEE THIS THING THAT HAS COME TO PASS, WHICH THE LORD HAS MADE KNOWN TO US." AND THEY CAME WITH HASTE AND FOUND MARY AND JOSEPH, AND THE BABE LYING IN A MANGER. NOW WHEN THEY HAD SEEN HIM, THEY MADE WIDELY KNOWN THE SAYING WHICH WAS TOLD THEM CONCERNING THIS CHILD. AND ALL THOSE WHO HEARD IT MARVELED AT THOSE THINGS WHICH WERE TOLD THEM BY THE SHEPHERDS. BUT MARY KEPT ALL THESE THINGS AND PONDERED THEM IN HER HEART.
~LUKE 2:15-19

ABIDING

Psalm 91:1 tells us, "He who dwells in the secret place of the Most High shall abide under the shadow of the Almighty." Do you know where the secret place was? It was in the sanctuary. Anytime you see "the secret place" you can just put "sanctuary."

> ONE THING I HAVE DESIRED OF THE LORD, THAT WILL I SEEK: THAT I MAY DWELL IN THE HOUSE OF THE LORD ALL THE DAYS OF MY LIFE, TO BEHOLD THE BEAUTY OF THE LORD, AND TO INQUIRE IN HIS TEMPLE.
> ~ PSALM 27:4

The Lord says this about the sanctuary:

> MAY HE SEND YOU HELP FROM THE SANCTUARY,
> AND STRENGTHEN YOU OUT OF ZION.
> ~ PSALM 20:2

> SO I HAVE LOOKED FOR YOU IN THE SANCTUARY,
> TO SEE YOUR POWER AND YOUR GLORY.
> ~ PSALM 63:2

> YOUR WAY, O GOD, IS IN THE SANCTUARY;
> WHO IS SO GREAT A GOD AS OUR GOD?
> ~ PSALM 77:13

> HONOR AND MAJESTY ARE BEFORE HIM;
> STRENGTH AND BEAUTY ARE IN HIS SANCTUARY.
> ~ PSALM 96:6

> "HEAVEN IS MY THRONE,
> AND THE EARTH IS MY FOOTSTOOL.
> WHERE IS THE HOUSE YOU WILL BUILD FOR ME?
> WHERE WILL MY RESTING PLACE BE?
> HAS NOT MY HAND MADE ALL THESE THINGS,
> AND SO THEY CAME INTO BEING?"
> DECLARES THE LORD.
> "THESE ARE THE ONES I LOOK ON WITH FAVOR:
> THOSE WHO ARE HUMBLE AND CONTRITE IN SPIRIT,
> AND WHO TREMBLE AT MY WORD."
> ~ ISAIAH 66:1–2 (NIV)

In John 4:23–24 Jesus gives clarification about worship and abiding in Him:

> BUT THE HOUR IS COMING, AND NOW IS, WHEN THE TRUE
> WORSHIPERS WILL WORSHIP THE FATHER IN SPIRIT AND
> TRUTH; FOR THE FATHER IS SEEKING SUCH TO WORSHIP
> HIM. GOD IS SPIRIT, AND THOSE WHO WORSHIP HIM
> MUST WORSHIP IN SPIRIT AND TRUTH.

The prophets of God had spoken about this new way to worship centuries earlier:

> "THE DAYS ARE COMING," SAYS THE LORD,
> "WHEN I WILL MAKE A NEW WAY OF WORSHIP FOR THE JEWS
> AND THOSE OF THE FAMILY GROUP OF JUDAH. THE NEW WAY
> OF WORSHIP WILL NOT BE LIKE THE OLD WAY OF WORSHIP I
> GAVE TO THEIR EARLY FATHERS. THAT WAS WHEN I TOOK THEM
> BY THE HAND AND LED THEM OUT OF EGYPT. BUT THEY DID
> NOT FOLLOW THE OLD WAY OF WORSHIP, EVEN WHEN I WAS A
> HUSBAND TO THEM," SAYS THE LORD. "THIS IS THE NEW WAY
> OF WORSHIP THAT I WILL GIVE TO THE JEWS. WHEN THAT DAY
> COMES," SAYS THE LORD, "I WILL PUT MY LAW INTO THEIR
> MINDS. AND I WILL WRITE IT ON THEIR HEARTS. I WILL BE THEIR
> GOD, AND THEY WILL BE MY PEOPLE."
> ~ JEREMIAH 31:31–33 (NLV)

> DO YOU NOT KNOW THAT YOUR BODY IS THE TEMPLE
> OF THE HOLY SPIRIT WHO IS IN YOU, WHOM YOU HAVE
> FROM GOD, AND YOU ARE NOT YOUR OWN?
> ~ 1 CORINTHIANS 6:19

We learn from these Scriptures that when we receive Christ's free gift of salvation, the Lord makes His sanctuary within us. His Holy Spirit then dwells within that inner sanctuary and teaches us, directs us, tells us, and reveals to us the greater things of God.

We no longer have to travel to a specific city or enter a specific building, but wherever we are we can enter into that secret place and abide with God. Christ within you—the hope of glory. Just as Jesus said, His Kingdom begins within you.

Abiding is something that happens as we seek the face of God, which the prophet Jeremiah describes in this way:

> THEN YOU WILL CALL UPON ME AND GO AND PRAY TO
> ME, AND I WILL LISTEN TO YOU. AND YOU WILL SEEK
> ME AND FIND ME, WHEN YOU SEARCH FOR ME WITH ALL
> YOUR HEART. I WILL BE FOUND BY YOU, SAYS THE LORD.
> ~ JEREMIAH 31:31-33

Although there are principles that need to be considered, abiding is not accomplished by applying a formula to achieve a goal. Abiding is a longing and an experience, not necessarily a goal.

A goal is something you set your focus on. "I've got to achieve this, and I've got to do this." If you set a goal while seeking the face of God, you'll find yourself *doing*. If you set a goal, you now have tasks to accomplish. But if you don't set a goal, if instead the goal remains a longing, your heart's cry will sound similar to this: "I long for His manifestation! I long to hear His voice! I long for His presence!" That is different than setting a goal, which can look like, "I will have His presence. I will find His presence. I will hear His voice." The goal causes you to *do*; the longing causes you to *be*. The goal makes you feel like a failure if it does not happen; the longing causes you to long more. It's the ever-present gift of His grace that draws you to long for Him.

We must embrace the reality that all the time we spend in meditation, in prayer, and in reading His Word requires complete dependence on God's Spirit flowing through us.

Here's a little secret: you can't spend a long time in prayer unless God is with you. You can do it in your own strength or will for five or ten minutes, and if you're really strong-willed, you might be able to do it for an hour. But you won't be able to do it day after day, nor will you walk away feeling refreshed. You'll walk away feeling you accomplished a task. You don't want *lectio divina* to be a task; you want to be refreshed. When you do it the right way, by dwelling in peace, you'll walk away feeling refreshed. You won't feel like you just finished a task—as if you should make another notch on your belt.

God's eternal Word will motivate us to pray as we read and practice it in our lives. We need to recognize that our prayer lives are the fountain from which all ministry flows. Psalm 55:17 declares, "Evening and morning and at noon I will pray, and cry aloud, and [God] shall hear my voice." Amen!

I cannot imagine a greater motivation to pray than that God enjoys having me in His presence. He enjoys my company. He delights in listening to me! He doesn't get bored with my repeated requests. He never makes me feel stupid. There is no rejection, only total acceptance.

R. T. Kendall

SEALING THE MOMENT—JOURNAL

When you practice *lectio divina*, it is important to write down what you experience. While journaling, you put into writing the precious treasures God spoke to you during this time of prayer. This seals the savor, the moment, the memory. It tells God that you value the experience and what He has said or might say.

> YOU SHALL WRITE [THE WORDS AND COMMANDS OF GOD] ON THE DOORPOSTS OF YOUR HOUSE AND ON YOUR GATES.
> ~ DEUTERONOMY 6:9

When you record what you observed with your five senses, you go from experiencing something to actually being in the moment. You keep it alive. When you commit it to writing, your muscles are moving, the bones are holding the pen, and the pen is flowing—it helps to seal what just took place during your time of prayer. It etches the moment in your memory. It goes beyond having the simple words on the page. You remember far more than you would have otherwise.

Sometimes the Lord may have you write out the particular verse or passage you prayed in its entirety. As you write it out, you may stumble across a word or phrase you wouldn't have recognized otherwise.

Later in this book, we've left space for you to journal your prayers and thoughts; however, it may be helpful to have a separate journal that is specific to this time of contemplative prayer.

twenty-two

WHERE DO I BEGIN?

The Word of God has 66 books (the New Jerusalem Bible has 73 because it includes Apocryphal writings), 1,189 chapters, and over 31,000 verses. Where does one begin to select a passage to pray?

OH, TASTE AND SEE THAT THE LORD IS GOOD.
~ PSALM 34:8

If you are currently reading through the Bible or studying a particular book, you can pick up where you last left off and begin *lectio divina* with the next passage.

If you are not currently reading through the Bible or any particular book, you can begin with some of the prayers that are already in the Bible. The Psalms are not only songs but prayers, and as mentioned earlier, they are often selected for *lectio divina*.

The book of Daniel is filled with prayers. In Daniel 2:20–23, we read the prayer Daniel prayed before he went to Nebuchadnezzar to interpret his dream. After Nebuchadnezzar is restored to sanity, he prays a blessing to the Most High God in 4:34–35. Daniel 9 is almost entirely a prayer.

In the New Testament, we find the prayers of Jesus. Here are a few examples:

THE LORD'S PRAYER:

OUR FATHER IN HEAVEN,
HALLOWED BE YOUR NAME.
YOUR KINGDOM COME.
YOUR WILL BE DONE

ON EARTH AS IT IS IN HEAVEN.
GIVE US THIS DAY OUR DAILY BREAD.
AND FORGIVE US OUR DEBTS,
AS WE FORGIVE OUR DEBTORS.
AND DO NOT LEAD US INTO TEMPTATION,
BUT DELIVER US FROM THE EVIL ONE.
FOR YOURS IS THE KINGDOM AND THE POWER
AND THE GLORY FOREVER. AMEN.
~ MATTHEW 6:9-13

There is the spontaneous praise/prayer of Jesus in Luke 10:21:

IN THAT HOUR JESUS REJOICED IN THE SPIRIT AND
SAID, "I THANK YOU, FATHER, LORD OF HEAVEN
AND EARTH, THAT YOU HAVE HIDDEN THESE THINGS
FROM THE WISE AND PRUDENT AND REVEALED THEM TO
BABES. EVEN SO, FATHER, FOR SO IT SEEMED GOOD IN
YOUR SIGHT."

The entire chapter of John 17 is a prayer Jesus prayed to the Father on the night before He went to the Cross, and it reveals His heart for those who are to come and follow Him.

Throughout the letters in the New Testament, you find various prayers Paul or other apostles prayed. These are sometimes referred to as Apostolic Prayers. Here are a few examples:

AND THIS I PRAY, THAT YOUR LOVE MAY ABOUND
STILL MORE AND MORE IN KNOWLEDGE AND ALL
DISCERNMENT, THAT YOU MAY APPROVE THE THINGS
THAT ARE EXCELLENT, THAT YOU MAY BE SINCERE
AND WITHOUT OFFENSE TILL THE DAY OF CHRIST,
BEING FILLED WITH THE FRUITS OF RIGHTEOUSNESS
WHICH ARE BY JESUS CHRIST, TO THE GLORY AND
PRAISE OF GOD.
~ PHILIPPIANS 1:9-11

THAT THE GOD OF OUR LORD JESUS CHRIST, THE
FATHER OF GLORY, MAY GIVE TO YOU THE SPIRIT OF
WISDOM AND REVELATION IN THE KNOWLEDGE OF
HIM, THE EYES OF YOUR UNDERSTANDING BEING
ENLIGHTENED; THAT YOU MAY KNOW WHAT IS THE HOPE
OF HIS CALLING, WHAT ARE THE RICHES OF THE GLORY
OF HIS INHERITANCE IN THE SAINTS, AND WHAT IS THE
EXCEEDING GREATNESS OF HIS POWER TOWARD US WHO
BELIEVE, ACCORDING TO THE WORKING OF HIS MIGHTY
POWER WHICH HE WORKED IN CHRIST WHEN HE
RAISED HIM FROM THE DEAD AND SEATED HIM AT HIS
RIGHT HAND IN THE HEAVENLY PLACES, FAR ABOVE ALL
PRINCIPALITY AND POWER AND MIGHT AND DOMINION,
AND EVERY NAME THAT IS NAMED, NOT ONLY IN THIS
AGE BUT ALSO IN THAT WHICH IS TO COME.
~ EPHESIANS 1:17-21

THEREFORE WE ALSO PRAY ALWAYS FOR YOU THAT OUR
GOD WOULD COUNT YOU WORTHY OF THIS CALLING, AND
FULFILL ALL THE GOOD PLEASURE OF HIS GOODNESS
AND THE WORK OF FAITH WITH POWER, THAT THE NAME
OF OUR LORD JESUS CHRIST MAY BE GLORIFIED IN YOU,
AND YOU IN HIM, ACCORDING TO THE GRACE OF OUR
GOD AND THE LORD JESUS CHRIST.
~ 2 THESSALONIANS 1:11-12

Take these passages and insert your own name, or "me," in those places where it says "you," and then begin to pray. "God, would You give *me* the spirit of wisdom and revelation in the knowledge of You? Jesus, would Your name be glorified in *me* according to Your grace?"

As you pray the Word of God more and more, you will find yourself more attuned to the Holy Spirit, who will lead you to read one passage or another.

Lectio Divina in a Group Setting

As I have previously written, while *lectio divina* is primarily a solitary and private method of prayer to connect the individual to the heart of God through His Word, there are times and places where this can be

THERE IS ONE BODY AND ONE SPIRIT, JUST AS YOU WERE CALLED IN ONE HOPE OF YOUR CALLING.

~ EPHESIANS 4:4

done in a group setting. When done within the same group over a period of weeks, months, or years, a tremendous trust and deep fellowship are developed among the participants.

It is ideal to have a group of four to eight participants during this time of prayer. One person should be the reader/leader of the group who oversees the sharing times.

Lectio divina, as a group practice, begins by selecting a verse or passage to be read during the allotted time, and then the leader reads the selected passage aloud. This should be done twice so that participants have a chance to grasp the idea of the verse before beginning their meditation and rumination on any particular phrase or word. The second time, the verse should be read slowly, pausing often, so that participants can hear and understand every word and phrase. Then there should be a time of silence and meditation, followed by a time of sharing. During the time of sharing, people can pray a particular portion of the verse or passage aloud, or they can share what touched their hearts.

Another participant should then read the same section of Scripture, once again reading it through slowly. Reading through a second time gives the participants the opportunity to "hear" and "see" Christ in the particular verse or passage.

The word that touched the participant's heart during the first reading is now turned into a question during the silent prayer: "Lord, why did that particular word or phrase stand out to me? What do You want me to see in my life? How do You want me to apply this word to my life today? Where or how am I in the way of what You want to do in my life?" It might be good to keep a pencil and paper close at hand, especially in the group practice of *lectio divina.*

A third participant, for voice difference and vocal inflection, should read through the passage a final time, once again reading it slowly and deliberately. This reading, and the silence and meditation that follow, is a time to engage with God about what He is calling you to do or be in the coming day or week ahead.

Afterward comes a time of sharing about how God is calling, speaking, or impressing each person.

When this final time of sharing is done, the group *lectio divina* might be concluded by each participant praying for the person on his or her right.

Jesus promised that when two or three of us are gathered in His name, He will be in the midst of us (Matthew 18:20). So although *lectio divina* is primarily a solitary form of prayer, meaning a single person in solitude and silence encountering the King of the Universe, there is great power when this is done in a group setting. Either way, we can still be assured of Jesus' presence.

twenty-four

MAKE AN APPOINTMENT WITH GOD

This is a powerful lesson. Spiritual disciplines are where the rubber meets the road, and talk becomes truth in your Christian walk. The world we live in has too many distractions. Even our distractions have distractions! You can watch streaming video on your phone and iPad that's delivered through the airwaves, and even that might be interrupted by a phone call.

IF YOU DILIGENTLY OBEY THE VOICE OF THE LORD YOUR GOD, TO OBSERVE CAREFULLY ALL HIS COMMANDMENTS WHICH I COMMAND YOU TODAY, THAT THE LORD YOUR GOD WILL SET YOU HIGH ABOVE ALL NATIONS OF THE EARTH.
~ DEUTERONOMY 28:1

Our obedience to open the Scriptures and spend time with the Lord releases a blessing in our lives. We have a promise from God of blessing. Provision is made in the promise, but through our actions we see the fulfillment of that promise.

BY MYSELF I HAVE SWORN, SAYS THE LORD, BECAUSE YOU HAVE DONE THIS THING, AND HAVE NOT WITHHELD YOUR SON, YOUR ONLY SON—BLESSING I WILL BLESS YOU, AND MULTIPLYING I WILL MULTIPLY YOUR DESCENDANTS AS THE STARS OF THE HEAVEN AND AS THE SAND WHICH IS ON THE SEASHORE; AND YOUR DESCENDANTS SHALL POSSESS THE GATE OF THEIR ENEMIES. IN YOUR SEED ALL THE NATIONS OF THE EARTH SHALL BE BLESSED, BECAUSE YOU HAVE OBEYED MY VOICE.
~ GENESIS 22:16-18

> WAS NOT ABRAHAM OUR FATHER JUSTIFIED BY WORKS
> WHEN HE OFFERED ISAAC HIS SON ON THE ALTAR? DO
> YOU SEE THAT FAITH WAS WORKING TOGETHER
> WITH HIS WORKS, AND BY WORKS FAITH WAS MADE
> PERFECT? AND THE SCRIPTURE WAS FULFILLED
> WHICH SAYS, "ABRAHAM BELIEVED GOD, AND IT WAS
> ACCOUNTED TO HIM FOR RIGHTEOUSNESS." AND HE WAS
> CALLED THE FRIEND OF GOD. YOU SEE THEN THAT A
> MAN IS JUSTIFIED BY WORKS, AND NOT BY FAITH ONLY.
> ~ JAMES 2:21-24

If you desire to hear the still, quiet voice of the Lord in today's world, you need to develop a habit of making an appointment with God. In this appointment with God, there are two things you can practice doing. First, meditate with a focus on His splendor and His glory; second, meditate on the Word of God by slowly and deliberately reading the Scriptures.

Develop this habit of meeting God in a place of peace and solitude, and you'll prepare your spirit to hear from Him in times of peace as well as times of crisis.

After you have been meditating in the Word and praying it out to God for some time, you will gradually find how easy it is to come into His presence. You will remember other Scriptures with less difficulty. Prayer has now become easy, sweet, and delightful.

Madame Guyon

twenty-five

THE PRACTICE OF DESIRE, DISCIPLINE, AND DELIGHT

Now that you have learned more about the art of praying the Scriptures and what *lectio divina* is, the process of preparation, and the benefits of it, this section of the book is intended to help you begin this practice.

> SO THEN FAITH COMES BY HEARING, AND HEARING BY THE WORD OF GOD.
> ~ ROMANS 10:17

On the pages that follow, you will find passages of Scripture I have taken the liberty to adapt for *lectio divina*. My intention is not to change Scripture but to personalize it. As you place yourself inside the truths here, *lectio divina* becomes a resource that makes engaging the Spirit of the Lord easier.

The truth of Scripture is true for everyone. Within that, it is true for you. This devotional is not intended to be a resource with which to study Scripture but rather to ingest Scripture, to allow it to interact with your imagination and your spirit—engendering the transformation I wrote about earlier.

The verses I included here should be a starting point. Hopefully after going through this devotional, you will come back to it again and again—but also open your Bible and find passages the Holy Spirit draws your attention to, and practice this spiritual discipline for the rest of your life.

I pray that you will encounter the Spirit of the living God as He makes His Word alive to you in brand-new ways, and in that encounter, you will be changed and transformed into the image of Jesus!

Lectio Divina Practice

You cannot be impatient and read the Bible. The practice of *lectio divina* is the unhurried savoring of the text so the eternal truths contained therein enter our spirits, and with that entrance we are more than changed—we are transformed. This "unhurried savoring" is a very important aspect of the transformation process.

The next portion of this book gives you the opportunity to practice the art of praying the Scriptures. On the following page, you will find a Study Card to help you through the process of *lectio divina*.

THE ART OF
praying
THE
SCRIPTURES

 HOOSE – *soul*
You can do one of these steps or all of them. You can enter a little or all the way. Your choice determines the depth of His response.

 REPARE – *body*
Relax your body and soul. Breathe in peace from the Holy Spirit.

 ECOGNIZE – *spirit*
God wants to commune with you. Loose your spirit to respond to that communion.

 ISTEN – *soul*
Come as you really are. You have no secrets from God—hold nothing back. Be completely honest and open with Him and yourself.

 EAD – *soul*
Read the Scripture slowly and deliberately in the presence of God. Place yourself in the passage or verse.

 RAY – *spirit*
Respond to His voice—repent, praise, respond, entreat. . .

 ONTEMPLATE – *spirit*
Think deeply, repeat words and phrases, ask God what He is saying while inviting His presence.

 BIDE – *body*
Rest in His love. Allow Him to wrap you in His love. Receive virtue from Heaven.

 OURNAL – *body*
Write down any new understanding or revelation you have received and how it might apply to you.

Walking in the Light

1 JOHN 1:5-10

THIS IS THE MESSAGE WHICH I HAVE HEARD FROM YOU, THAT YOU, GOD, ARE LIGHT, AND IN YOU IS NO DARKNESS AT ALL. IF I SAY THAT I HAVE FELLOWSHIP WITH YOU, AND WALK IN DARKNESS, I LIE AND DO NOT PRACTICE THE TRUTH. BUT IF I WALK IN THE LIGHT AS YOU ARE IN THE LIGHT, I HAVE FELLOWSHIP WITH THE BODY OF CHRIST, AND THE BLOOD OF JESUS CHRIST YOUR SON CLEANSES ME FROM ALL SIN. IF I SAY THAT I HAVE NO SIN, I DECEIVE MYSELF, AND THE TRUTH IS NOT IN ME. IF I CONFESS MY SINS, YOU ARE FAITHFUL AND JUST TO FORGIVE ME OF MY SINS AND TO CLEANSE ME FROM ALL UNRIGHTEOUSNESS. IF I SAY THAT I HAVE NOT SINNED, I MAKE YOU A LIAR, AND YOUR WORD IS NOT IN ME.

Sit in silence for a couple of minutes and allow yourself to think about whatever parts of this Scripture stand out to you. When your mind begins to wander, read the Scripture again slowly, and see if anything else grabs your attention or imagination. Repeat until nothing else stands out. Make notes in the space below (or in a separate journal) to record what stands out to you.

Engage the Lord in prayer over the thoughts you have recorded. When you finish, go to the next page.

Pray each of the thoughts below back to the Lord. Take time with each one. If more thoughts come as you pray, write them down, either in the space provided or in a separate journal.

I have heard the same message Christ delivered to His apostles when He walked the earth after His resurrection.

The message is that You are light and there is nothing dark in You. There is nothing dark that even causes a shadow in Your being. You are perfect light!

I walk in the light because I have the light—Christ Jesus in me.

Having the light and walking in the light cause me to have fellowship with other believers—I am part of the Body of Christ.

It is Your blood that cleanses me from all sin.

I know my sinfulness, and this draws me closer to You because I do not hide my sin. I confess my sin, and You forgive me.

You not only forgive me, but You cleanse me from all unrighteousness.

Lord, I know Your Word is in me and Your Word is true. Continue to cause Your light to shine more brightly within me and remove anything that would hinder Your light from shining through me!

What was the main thing the Lord spoke to you or changed in you through this meditation?

Christ—the Word and the Light

JOHN 1:1-5, 9-13

IN THE BEGINNING WAS THE WORD, AND THE WORD WAS WITH GOD, AND THE WORD WAS GOD. YOU WERE IN THE BEGINNING WITH GOD.

ALL THINGS WERE MADE THROUGH YOU, AND WITHOUT YOU NOTHING WAS MADE THAT WAS MADE. IN YOU WAS LIFE, AND THE LIFE WAS THE LIGHT OF MEN. AND THE LIGHT SHINES IN THE DARKNESS, AND THE DARKNESS DID NOT COMPREHEND IT. THAT WAS THE TRUE LIGHT WHICH, COMING INTO THE WORLD, GIVES LIGHT TO EVERY MAN. YOU WERE IN THE WORLD, AND THE WORLD WAS MADE THROUGH YOU, AND THE WORLD DID NOT KNOW YOU. YOU CAME TO YOUR OWN, AND YOUR OWN DID NOT RECEIVE YOU. BUT WHEN I RECEIVED YOU, YOU GAVE ME THE RIGHT TO BECOME A CHILD OF GOD, BECAUSE I BELIEVE IN YOUR NAME, AND SO I WAS BORN, NOT OF BLOOD, NOR OF THE WILL OF THE FLESH, NOR OF THE WILL OF MAN, BUT OF GOD.

Sit in silence for a couple of minutes and allow yourself to think about whatever parts of this Scripture stand out to you. When your mind begins to wander, read the Scripture again slowly, and see if anything else grabs your attention or imagination. Repeat until nothing else stands out. Make notes in the space below (or in a separate journal) to record what stands out to you.

Engage the Lord in prayer over the thoughts you have recorded. When you finish, go to the next page.

Pray each of the thoughts below back to the Lord. Take time with each one. If more thoughts come as you pray, write them down, either in the space provided or in a separate journal.

You have always been. You completely communicate who God is because You are God.

You made all things, including me. I was formed by You.

In You is the fullness of life—abundant life—and that life is the light in me. Before I knew You, I didn't understand this light; I couldn't comprehend it, but now I know You—the Light of the world.

Even though You made all things, many do not know You, and many have not received You. Thank You for allowing me to receive You!

Because You gave me faith to receive You, I am Your child. I exist, not because of my parents or any other thing but because You wanted *me* to exist. I am Yours because You wanted *me*. Thank You!

What was the main thing the Lord spoke to you or changed in you through this meditation?

Wisdom—
Christ as Wisdom Personified

PROVERBS 8:22–31

THE LORD POSSESSED ME AT THE BEGINNING OF HIS WAY,
BEFORE HIS WORKS OF OLD.
I HAVE BEEN ESTABLISHED FROM EVERLASTING,
FROM THE BEGINNING,
BEFORE THERE WAS EVER AN EARTH.
WHEN THERE WERE NO DEPTHS I WAS BROUGHT FORTH,
WHEN THERE WERE NO FOUNTAINS ABOUNDING WITH WATER.
BEFORE THE MOUNTAINS WERE SETTLED,
BEFORE THE HILLS, I WAS BROUGHT FORTH;
WHILE AS YET HE HAD NOT MADE THE EARTH OR THE FIELDS,
OR THE PRIMAL DUST OF THE WORLD.
WHEN HE PREPARED THE HEAVENS, I WAS THERE,
WHEN HE DREW A CIRCLE ON THE FACE OF THE DEEP,
WHEN HE ESTABLISHED THE CLOUDS ABOVE,
WHEN HE STRENGTHENED THE FOUNTAINS OF THE DEEP,
WHEN HE ASSIGNED TO THE SEA ITS LIMIT,
SO THAT THE WATERS WOULD NOT TRANSGRESS HIS COMMAND,
WHEN HE MARKED OUT THE FOUNDATIONS OF THE EARTH,
THEN I WAS BESIDE HIM AS A MASTER CRAFTSMAN;
AND I WAS DAILY HIS DELIGHT,
REJOICING ALWAYS BEFORE HIM,
REJOICING IN HIS INHABITED WORLD,
AND MY DELIGHT WAS WITH THE SONS OF MEN.

Sit in silence for a couple of minutes and allow yourself to think about whatever parts of this Scripture stand out to you. When your mind begins to wander, read the Scripture again slowly, and see if anything else grabs your attention or imagination. Repeat until nothing else stands out. Make notes in the space below (or in a separate journal) to record what stands out to you.

Engage the Lord in prayer over the thoughts you have recorded. When you finish, go to the next page.

Pray each of the thoughts below back to the Lord. Take time with each one. If more thoughts come as you pray, write them down, either in the space provided or in a separate journal.

Wisdom is the foundation of everything You have done and will do.

Wisdom was with You when You formed all creation, so all creation reveals Your wisdom. Give me eyes to see Your wisdom in creation.

Wisdom is a person, a master creation, and wisdom personified gives great joy to the Father.

Wisdom delights in the sons of men. Wisdom delights in me!

You delight in wisdom; cause me to delight in wisdom the same way You do!

Lord, Your Word says that You give wisdom to anyone who asks. Give me the wisdom You delight in.

What was the main thing the Lord spoke to you or changed in you through this meditation?

The Living Word and Great High Priest

HEBREWS 4:11–16

LET ME THEREFORE BE DILIGENT TO ENTER THAT REST, LEST I
FALL ACCORDING TO THE SAME EXAMPLE OF DISOBEDIENCE. FOR
YOUR WORD, GOD, IS LIVING AND POWERFUL, AND SHARPER
THAN ANY TWO-EDGED SWORD, PIERCING EVEN TO THE DIVISION
OF SOUL AND SPIRIT, AND OF JOINTS AND MARROW, AND IS A
DISCERNER OF THE THOUGHTS AND INTENTS OF THE HEART,
EVEN MY HEART. AND THERE IS NO CREATURE HIDDEN FROM
YOUR SIGHT, BUT ALL THINGS ARE NAKED AND OPEN TO YOUR
EYES, THE ONE TO WHOM I MUST GIVE ACCOUNT. SEEING THEN
THAT I HAVE A GREAT HIGH PRIEST WHO HAS PASSED THROUGH
THE HEAVENS, JESUS, THE SON OF GOD, LET ME HOLD FAST MY
CONFESSION. FOR I DO NOT HAVE A HIGH PRIEST WHO CANNOT
SYMPATHIZE WITH MY WEAKNESSES, BUT WAS IN ALL POINTS
TEMPTED AS I AM, YET WITHOUT SIN. LET ME THEREFORE COME
BOLDLY TO THE THRONE OF GRACE, THAT I MAY OBTAIN MERCY
AND FIND GRACE TO HELP IN TIME OF NEED.

Sit in silence for a couple of minutes and allow yourself to think about whatever parts of this Scripture stand out to you. When your mind begins to wander, read the Scripture again slowly, and see if anything else grabs your attention or imagination. Repeat until nothing else stands out. Make notes in the space below (or in a separate journal) to record what stands out to you.

Engage the Lord in prayer over the thoughts you have recorded. When you finish, go to the next page.

Pray each of the thoughts below back to the Lord. Take time with each one. If more thoughts come as you pray, write them down, either in the space provided or in a separate journal.

Teach me how rest prepares me to receive Your Word.

Use Your Word to pierce to the division of my soul, my spirit, and my body. Show me which thoughts and intents of my heart are from the soul and which are from the spirit.

Lord, I know You are the Word. Allow Your life in me to rise up so that I walk according to Your Spirit. Cut away all thoughts and intents that are based on what I think, what I feel, and what I want. I surrender my soul to You.

You know everything I go through. You understand. You know my weaknesses, and You sympathize. Give me Your strength to overcome temptation like You did.

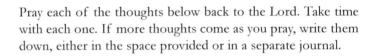

Because of who You are and what You have done, I come boldly. I need mercy! I need grace! This is my time of need. Hear my prayer.

Lord, I am humbled that I can come to Your throne. Thank You for sending Jesus to open a way to You.

What was the main thing the Lord spoke to you or changed in you through this meditation?

The Father Chose Me as a Son

EPHESIANS 1:3-12

BLESSED BE THE GOD AND FATHER OF MY LORD JESUS CHRIST, WHO HAS BLESSED ME WITH EVERY SPIRITUAL BLESSING IN THE HEAVENLY PLACES IN CHRIST, JUST AS HE CHOSE ME IN HIM BEFORE THE FOUNDATION OF THE WORLD, THAT I SHOULD BE HOLY AND WITHOUT BLAME BEFORE HIM IN LOVE, HAVING PREDESTINED ME TO ADOPTION AS A SON/DAUGHTER BY JESUS CHRIST TO HIMSELF, ACCORDING TO THE GOOD PLEASURE OF HIS WILL, TO THE PRAISE OF THE GLORY OF HIS GRACE, BY WHICH HE MADE ME ACCEPTED IN THE BELOVED.

IN HIM I HAVE REDEMPTION THROUGH HIS BLOOD, THE FORGIVENESS OF SINS, ACCORDING TO THE RICHES OF HIS GRACE WHICH HE MADE TO ABOUND TOWARD ME IN ALL WISDOM AND PRUDENCE, HAVING MADE KNOWN TO ME THE MYSTERY OF HIS WILL, ACCORDING TO HIS GOOD PLEASURE WHICH HE PURPOSED IN HIMSELF, THAT IN THE DISPENSATION OF THE FULLNESS OF THE TIMES HE MIGHT GATHER TOGETHER IN ONE ALL THINGS IN CHRIST, BOTH WHICH ARE IN HEAVEN AND WHICH ARE ON EARTH—IN HIM. IN HIM ALSO I HAVE OBTAINED AN INHERITANCE, BEING PREDESTINED ACCORDING TO THE PURPOSE OF HIM WHO WORKS ALL THINGS ACCORDING TO THE COUNSEL OF HIS WILL, THAT I WHO TRUSTED IN CHRIST SHOULD BE TO THE PRAISE OF HIS GLORY.

Sit in silence for a couple of minutes and allow yourself to think about whatever parts of this Scripture stand out to you. When your mind begins to wander, read the Scripture again slowly, and see if anything else grabs your attention or imagination. Repeat until nothing else stands out. Make notes in the space below (or in a separate journal) to record what stands out to you.

Engage the Lord in prayer over the thoughts you have recorded. When you finish, go to the next page.

Pray each of the thoughts below back to the Lord. Take time with each one. If more thoughts come as you pray, write them down, either in the space provided or in a separate journal.

You have blessed me with every spiritual blessing. Reveal to me what those blessings are.

Before the foundation of the world, You chose me for love. You chose me to be Your child. This gives You pleasure.

I am accepted because I am in Your Beloved; I am in Christ who redeemed me.

In You I am forgiven, and You make known to me the mystery of Your will. Tell me Your will.

I am Your child, and as Your child I have an inheritance. Part of my inheritance is bringing You praise and revealing Your glory. Show me more of this inheritance.

Father, thank You for choosing me. Help settle my heart in this reality. Make it experiential for me.

What was the main thing the Lord spoke to you or changed in you through this meditation?

I am Filled, Circumcised, Buried, and Made Alive in Christ

COLOSSIANS 2:8-15

I NEED TO BEWARE LEST ANYONE CHEAT ME THROUGH PHILOSOPHY AND EMPTY DECEIT, ACCORDING TO THE TRADITION OF MEN, ACCORDING TO THE BASIC PRINCIPLES OF THE WORLD, AND NOT ACCORDING TO CHRIST. FOR IN YOU DWELLS ALL THE FULLNESS OF THE GODHEAD BODILY, AND I AM COMPLETE IN YOU. YOU ARE THE HEAD OF ALL PRINCIPALITY AND POWER.

IN YOU I WAS ALSO CIRCUMCISED WITH THE CIRCUMCISION MADE WITHOUT HANDS, BY PUTTING OFF THE BODY OF THE SINS OF THE FLESH, BY THE CIRCUMCISION OF CHRIST, BURIED WITH YOU IN BAPTISM, IN WHICH I WAS ALSO RAISED WITH YOU THROUGH FAITH IN THE WORKING OF GOD, WHO RAISED YOU FROM THE DEAD. AND I, BEING DEAD IN MY TRESPASSES AND THE UNCIRCUMCISION OF MY FLESH, WAS MADE ALIVE TOGETHER WITH YOU. YOU FORGAVE ME ALL MY TRESPASSES AND WIPED OUT THE HANDWRITING OF REQUIREMENTS THAT WAS AGAINST ME, WHICH WAS CONTRARY TO ME. AND YOU HAVE TAKEN IT OUT OF THE WAY, HAVING NAILED IT TO THE CROSS. HAVING DISARMED PRINCIPALITIES AND POWERS, YOU MADE A PUBLIC SPECTACLE OF THEM, TRIUMPHING OVER THEM IN IT.

Sit in silence for a couple of minutes and allow yourself to think about whatever parts of this Scripture stand out to you. When your mind begins to wander, read the Scripture again slowly, and see if anything else grabs your attention or imagination. Repeat until nothing else stands out. Make notes in the space below (or in a separate journal) to record what stands out to you.

Engage the Lord in prayer over the thoughts you have recorded. When you finish, go to the next page.

Pray each of the thoughts below back to the Lord. Take time with each one. If more thoughts come as you pray, write them down, either in the space provided or in a separate journal.

Show me how to guard my heart against philosophy, empty deceit, traditions of men, and the elemental principles of the world.

All of God is in You, and You are in me.

You circumcised my heart, buried me in baptism, and gave me new life by faith in God's power to raise the dead. Give me more faith!

You have completely wiped out the debt I owed. You nailed it to the Cross. Help me to see my old nature, my old habits, and my old man nailed to the Cross.

When You rose from the dead, You declared to all creation that You are head over all. You disarmed all powers. You are triumphant!

.

Jesus, thank You for dying and for rising from the grave. Thank You for including me in Your victory!

What was the main thing the Lord spoke to you or changed in you through this meditation?

Think on These Things

Philippians 4:4-9

I will rejoice in the Lord always. Again I will say, rejoice!

Let my gentleness be known to all men. You, Lord, are at hand. I will be anxious for nothing, but in everything by prayer and supplication, with thanksgiving, I will let my requests be made known to You; and Your peace, which surpasses all understanding, will guard my heart and mind through Christ Jesus.

Finally, whatever things are true, whatever things are noble, whatever things are just, whatever things are pure, whatever things are lovely, whatever things are of good report, if there is any virtue and if there is anything praiseworthy—I will meditate on these things. The things which I learned and received and heard and saw in others, these I will do, and the God of peace will be with me.

Sit in silence for a couple of minutes and allow yourself to think about whatever parts of this Scripture stand out to you. When your mind begins to wander, read the Scripture again slowly, and see if anything else grabs your attention or imagination. Repeat until nothing else stands out. Make notes in the space below (or in a separate journal) to record what stands out to you.

Engage the Lord in prayer over the thoughts you have recorded. When you finish, go to the next page.

Pray each of the thoughts below back to the Lord. Take time with each one. If more thoughts come as you pray, write them down, either in the space provided or in a separate journal.

The position of my heart is rejoicing. I choose to rejoice. Heart, I command you to rejoice in God!

Because I know You are near, I do not have to fight, struggle, or demand my way. My gentleness will be seen by everyone who meets me.

I trust You. I can tell You what I need and let go of my need to control and manipulate. I will not be anxious. I have peace, knowing You are good and You are for me.

I will make the true, noble, just, pure, lovely, virtuous, and praiseworthy things—things of good report—my meditation. I will not meditate on the negative; I will meditate on the good!

Lord, You are true, noble, just, pure, lovely, virtuous, and praiseworthy. You are the "good report." I choose to meditate on You.

Thank You for being with me. Let my heart be settled in Your peace, knowing You are always with me.

What was the main thing the Lord spoke to you or changed in you through this meditation?

Counting All Things Loss to Know Him

PHILIPPIANS 3:7-14

BUT WHAT THINGS WERE GAIN TO ME, THESE I HAVE COUNTED
LOSS FOR CHRIST. YET INDEED I ALSO COUNT ALL THINGS
LOSS FOR THE EXCELLENCE OF THE KNOWLEDGE OF YOU,
CHRIST JESUS MY LORD, FOR WHOM I HAVE SUFFERED THE
LOSS OF ALL THINGS, AND COUNT THEM AS RUBBISH, THAT I
MAY GAIN YOU AND BE FOUND IN YOU, NOT HAVING MY OWN
RIGHTEOUSNESS, WHICH IS FROM THE LAW, BUT THAT WHICH
IS THROUGH FAITH IN YOU, THE RIGHTEOUSNESS WHICH IS
FROM GOD BY FAITH; THAT I MAY KNOW YOU AND THE POWER
OF YOUR RESURRECTION AND THE FELLOWSHIP OF YOUR
SUFFERINGS, BEING CONFORMED TO YOUR DEATH, IF, BY ANY
MEANS, I MAY ATTAIN TO THE RESURRECTION FROM THE DEAD.

NOT THAT I HAVE ALREADY ATTAINED OR AM ALREADY
PERFECTED, BUT I PRESS ON, THAT I MAY LAY HOLD OF THAT
FOR WHICH YOU HAVE ALSO LAID HOLD OF ME. I DO NOT
COUNT MYSELF TO HAVE APPREHENDED, BUT ONE THING I DO,
FORGETTING THOSE THINGS WHICH ARE BEHIND AND REACHING
FORWARD TO THOSE THINGS WHICH ARE AHEAD. I PRESS
TOWARD THE GOAL FOR THE PRIZE OF THE UPWARD CALL OF
GOD IN YOU—CHRIST JESUS.

Sit in silence for a couple of minutes and allow yourself to think about whatever parts of this Scripture stand out to you. When your mind begins to wander, read the Scripture again slowly, and see if anything else grabs your attention or imagination. Repeat until nothing else stands out. Make notes in the space below (or in a separate journal) to record what stands out to you.

Engage the Lord in prayer over the thoughts you have recorded. When you finish, go to the next page.

Pray each of the thoughts below back to the Lord. Take time with each one. If more thoughts come as you pray, write them down, either in the space provided or in a separate journal.

Show me anything of the world I have considered to be "gain." Show me how to value knowing You more.

Show me how to consider anything that does not draw me closer to You as rubbish, garbage, and filth.

It is not my accomplishments, my abilities, or even my desire to do right that allows me to come to You—it is what Jesus did. I trust in Your righteousness, not mine.

I want to know Your power, so I accept Your sufferings and Your death. Kill anything in me that hinders Your resurrection power working through me and in me.

I know I am not perfect yet, but I refuse to place my attention on that. I press on to the goal. You are the goal. You are my "very great reward."

Father, thank You for calling me and giving me faith so that I can be united with Christ in His death and life.

What was the main thing the Lord spoke to you or changed in you through this meditation?

The Lord Calls, Equips, Keeps, and Anoints – Declaring What Is to Come

ISAIAH 42:5-9

THUS SAYS GOD THE LORD,
WHO CREATED THE HEAVENS AND STRETCHED THEM OUT,
WHO SPREAD FORTH THE EARTH AND
THAT WHICH COMES FROM IT,
WHO GIVES BREATH TO THE PEOPLE ON IT,
AND SPIRIT TO THOSE WHO WALK ON IT:
"I, THE LORD, HAVE CALLED YOU IN RIGHTEOUSNESS,
AND WILL HOLD YOUR HAND;
I WILL KEEP YOU AND GIVE YOU AS A COVENANT TO THE
PEOPLE, AS A LIGHT TO THE GENTILES,
TO OPEN BLIND EYES,
TO BRING OUT PRISONERS FROM THE PRISON,
THOSE WHO SIT IN DARKNESS FROM THE PRISON HOUSE.
I AM THE LORD, THAT IS MY NAME;
AND MY GLORY I WILL NOT GIVE TO ANOTHER,
NOR MY PRAISE TO CARVED IMAGES.
BEHOLD, THE FORMER THINGS HAVE COME TO PASS,
AND NEW THINGS I DECLARE;
BEFORE THEY SPRING FORTH I TELL YOU OF THEM."

Sit in silence for a couple of minutes and allow yourself to think about whatever parts of this Scripture stand out to you. When your mind begins to wander, read the Scripture again slowly, and see if anything else grabs your attention or imagination. Repeat until nothing else stands out. Make notes in the space below (or in a separate journal) to record what stands out to you.

Engage the Lord in prayer over the thoughts you have recorded. When you finish, go to the next page.

Pray each of the thoughts below back to the Lord. Take time with each one. If more thoughts come as you pray, write them down, either in the space provided or in a separate journal.

You created all things. You made the earth. You made me. Your breath gives spirit to all flesh.

You called me. You hold my hand. You have sent me to the nations.

Because You are with me and because I carry Jesus, I carry Your light to the nations. I open blind eyes. I set prisoners free from darkness and show them the Light.

You, the Creator, do these things because it is Your will and You receive glory. Father, receive glory from my life.

You declare all things before they come to pass. You have said these things about me, so they *will* come to pass.

Father, thank You for declaring new things over my life, over my nation, and over the world. Let me hear the new thing You are saying right now.

What was the main thing the Lord spoke to you or changed in you through this meditation?

God's Righteousness Through Faith

ROMANS 3:21–26

BUT NOW THE RIGHTEOUSNESS OF GOD APART FROM THE
LAW IS REVEALED, BEING WITNESSED BY THE LAW AND THE
PROPHETS, EVEN THE RIGHTEOUSNESS OF GOD, THROUGH FAITH
IN JESUS CHRIST, TO ALL AND ON ALL WHO BELIEVE, EVEN ME.
FOR THERE IS NO DIFFERENCE; FOR ALL HAVE SINNED AND FALL
SHORT OF THE GLORY OF GOD, BEING JUSTIFIED FREELY BY HIS
GRACE THROUGH THE REDEMPTION THAT IS IN CHRIST JESUS,
WHOM GOD SET FORTH AS A PROPITIATION BY HIS BLOOD,
THROUGH FAITH, TO DEMONSTRATE HIS RIGHTEOUSNESS.
BECAUSE IN HIS FORBEARANCE GOD HAD PASSED OVER THE
SINS THAT WERE PREVIOUSLY COMMITTED, TO DEMONSTRATE
AT THE PRESENT TIME HIS RIGHTEOUSNESS, THAT HE MIGHT BE
JUST AND THE JUSTIFIER OF THE ONE WHO HAS FAITH IN JESUS.

Sit in silence for a couple of minutes and allow yourself to think about whatever parts of this Scripture stand out to you. When your mind begins to wander, read the Scripture again slowly, and see if anything else grabs your attention or imagination. Repeat until nothing else stands out. Make notes in the space below (or in a separate journal) to record what stands out to you.

Engage the Lord in prayer over the thoughts you have recorded. When you finish, go to the next page.

Pray each of the thoughts below back to the Lord. Take time with each one. If more thoughts come as you pray, write them down, either in the space provided or in a separate journal.

Righteousness for me does not rest on my ability to do the right thing. I failed. But You still declare me righteous. Wow!

My faith in what You have done is actually Your faith. It is Your faith giving me faith. It is all about You!

You have redeemed me. Your blood covered all my wickedness, and Your righteousness is shown.

You had to die. My sins made it necessary. They had to be covered. You wanted to die. Your love made that necessary. You love me that much.

I can take no credit for the love I have for You. I can take no credit for my desire to be right before You.

Jesus, thank You for demonstrating Your righteousness, forbearance, and patience in me!

What was the main thing the Lord spoke to you or changed in you through this meditation?

A Vision of the Throne of God

Revelation 4:1-4

After these things I looked, and behold, a door standing open in Heaven. And the first voice which I heard was like a trumpet speaking with me, saying, "Come up here, and I will show you things which must take place after this."

Immediately I was in the Spirit; and behold, a throne set in Heaven, and One sat on the throne. And He who sat there was like a jasper and a sardius stone in appearance; and there was a rainbow around the throne, in appearance like an emerald. Around the throne were twenty-four thrones, and on the thrones I saw twenty-four elders sitting, clothed in white robes; and they had crowns of gold on their heads.

Sit in silence for a couple of minutes and allow yourself to think about whatever parts of this Scripture stand out to you. When your mind begins to wander, read the Scripture again slowly, and see if anything else grabs your attention or imagination. Repeat until nothing else stands out. Make notes in the space below (or in a separate journal) to record what stands out to you.

Engage the Lord in prayer over the thoughts you have recorded. When you finish, go to the next page.

Pray each of the thoughts below back to the Lord. Take time with each one. If more thoughts come as you pray, write them down, either in the space provided or in a separate journal.

Father, only You can open that door. I ask that You allow me to hear that voice and go through that door when You know I am ready.

Would You show me the things to come? Will You tell me what is soon going to take place?

Let me see Your radiance and Your beauty, the rainbow around Your throne, the lights and the colors. Give me eyes to see You!

You are sitting on Your eternal throne. You are reigning. You are King. Look at my life and reign in my circumstances.

Who are the twenty-four elders? Why are they on thrones? Why are their robes white? Why do they wear crowns? Teach me heavenly things, Lord.

Jesus, thank You for opening a way into the Holy Place in Heaven through the veil that is Your flesh. I believe.

What was the main thing the Lord spoke to you or changed in you through this meditation?

"I Am Willing—
Be Cleansed"

MARK 1:40-42

NOW A LEPER CAME TO HIM, IMPLORING HIM, KNEELING DOWN
TO HIM, AND SAYING TO HIM, "IF YOU ARE WILLING, YOU CAN
MAKE ME CLEAN." THEN JESUS, MOVED WITH COMPASSION,
STRETCHED OUT HIS HAND AND TOUCHED HIM, AND SAID TO
HIM, "I AM WILLING; BE CLEANSED." AS SOON AS HE HAD
SPOKEN, IMMEDIATELY THE LEPROSY LEFT HIM, AND HE WAS
CLEANSED.

Sit in silence for a couple of minutes and allow yourself to think about whatever parts of this Scripture stand out to you. When your mind begins to wander, read the Scripture again slowly, and see if anything else grabs your attention or imagination. Repeat until nothing else stands out. Make notes in the space below (or in a separate journal) to record what stands out to you.

Engage the Lord in prayer over the thoughts you have recorded. When you finish, go to the next page.

Pray each of the thoughts below back to the Lord. Take time with each one. If more thoughts come as you pray, write them down, either in the space provided or in a separate journal.

God, sometimes I wonder if You want to move in the circumstances I face. Speak to me.

I feel I am like this leper—unclean and outcast, but You can make me clean.

Help me to grasp Your compassion over my situation. Show me how much You care for me.

Give me that same compassion for those I meet, especially those who are the most broken and despised by man. I am willing, Lord.

Immediately the leprosy left me. Immediately I was made clean. You do a complete, thorough work in me.

Father, thank You for giving me a window into Your heart with Jesus' response. Make me just like You!

What was the main thing the Lord spoke to you or changed in you through this meditation?

"Neither Do I Condemn You"

JOHN 8:3-11

THEN THE SCRIBES AND PHARISEES BROUGHT TO HIM A WOMAN
CAUGHT IN ADULTERY. AND WHEN THEY HAD SET HER IN THE
MIDST, THEY SAID TO HIM, "TEACHER, THIS WOMAN WAS
CAUGHT IN ADULTERY, IN THE VERY ACT. NOW MOSES, IN THE
LAW, COMMANDED US THAT SUCH SHOULD BE STONED. BUT
WHAT DO YOU SAY?" THIS THEY SAID, TESTING HIM, THAT THEY
MIGHT HAVE SOMETHING OF WHICH TO ACCUSE HIM. BUT JESUS
STOOPED DOWN AND WROTE ON THE GROUND WITH HIS FINGER,
AS THOUGH HE DID NOT HEAR.

SO WHEN THEY CONTINUED ASKING HIM, HE RAISED HIMSELF
UP AND SAID TO THEM, "HE WHO IS WITHOUT SIN AMONG
YOU, LET HIM THROW A STONE AT HER FIRST." AND AGAIN HE
STOOPED DOWN AND WROTE ON THE GROUND. THEN THOSE WHO
HEARD IT, BEING CONVICTED BY THEIR CONSCIENCE, WENT OUT
ONE BY ONE, BEGINNING WITH THE OLDEST EVEN TO THE LAST.
AND JESUS WAS LEFT ALONE, AND THE WOMAN STANDING IN
THE MIDST. WHEN JESUS HAD RAISED HIMSELF UP AND SAW NO
ONE BUT THE WOMAN, HE SAID TO HER, "WOMAN, WHERE ARE
THOSE ACCUSERS OF YOURS? HAS NO ONE CONDEMNED YOU?"
SHE SAID, "NO ONE, LORD." AND JESUS SAID TO HER, "NEITHER
DO I CONDEMN YOU; GO AND SIN NO MORE."

Sit in silence for a couple of minutes and allow yourself to think about whatever parts of this Scripture stand out to you. When your mind begins to wander, read the Scripture again slowly, and see if anything else grabs your attention or imagination. Repeat until nothing else stands out. Make notes in the space below (or in a separate journal) to record what stands out to you.

Engage the Lord in prayer over the thoughts you have recorded. When you finish, go to the next page.

Pray each of the thoughts below back to the Lord. Take time with each one. If more thoughts come as you pray, write them down, either in the space provided or in a separate journal.

I am the woman caught in the act. I have sinned. I deserve to die. I deserve judgment. What is Your response to my sin?

I am the one wanting to throw stones. I accuse my brothers and sisters. I notice their sin and wish they would get caught. Forgive me, Father. Help me to see.

Give me the wisdom to walk away when others accuse people. Convict my conscience, Lord. Teach me mercy!

You wait. I don't understand Your silence, but You are waiting to have mercy. Help me to have faith in the waiting.

You are the One who justifies; who can condemn? When You stand, no one can condemn me. What grace!

Jesus, I receive Your forgiveness. Give me grace (power that is not mine) to go and sin no more.

What was the main thing the Lord spoke to you or changed in you through this meditation?

A Vision of the Risen Christ

REVELATION 1:12-18

THEN I TURNED TO SEE THE VOICE THAT SPOKE WITH ME. AND HAVING TURNED I SAW SEVEN GOLDEN LAMPSTANDS, AND IN THE MIDST OF THE SEVEN LAMPSTANDS ONE LIKE THE SON OF MAN, CLOTHED WITH A GARMENT DOWN TO THE FEET AND GIRDED ABOUT THE CHEST WITH A GOLDEN BAND. HIS HEAD AND HAIR WERE WHITE LIKE WOOL, AS WHITE AS SNOW, AND HIS EYES LIKE A FLAME OF FIRE; HIS FEET WERE LIKE FINE BRASS, AS IF REFINED IN A FURNACE, AND HIS VOICE AS THE SOUND OF MANY WATERS; HE HAD IN HIS RIGHT HAND SEVEN STARS, OUT OF HIS MOUTH WENT A SHARP TWO-EDGED SWORD, AND HIS COUNTENANCE WAS LIKE THE SUN SHINING IN ITS STRENGTH. AND WHEN I SAW HIM, I FELL AT HIS FEET AS DEAD. BUT HE LAID HIS RIGHT HAND ON ME, SAYING TO ME, "DO NOT BE AFRAID; I AM THE FIRST AND THE LAST. I AM HE WHO LIVES, AND WAS DEAD, AND BEHOLD, I AM ALIVE FOREVERMORE. AMEN. AND I HAVE THE KEYS OF HADES AND OF DEATH."

Sit in silence for a couple of minutes and allow yourself to think about whatever parts of this Scripture stand out to you. When your mind begins to wander, read the Scripture again slowly, and see if anything else grabs your attention or imagination. Repeat until nothing else stands out. Make notes in the space below (or in a separate journal) to record what stands out to you.

Engage the Lord in prayer over the thoughts you have recorded. When you finish, go to the next page.

Pray each of the thoughts below back to the Lord. Take time with each one. If more thoughts come as you pray, write them down, either in the space provided or in a separate journal.

You stand in the midst of seven golden lampstands. The Light of the world stands in the midst of the light.

Your hair is white, pure, and undefiled. Your eyes are fire, burning with desire. Let me see You.

Your voice—oh, that awesome voice—sounds like waters, thundering in its power. Let me hear You.

You shine like the sun. Your brilliance is overwhelming. If You do not strengthen me, I cannot stand in the presence of such holiness.

Yet in the midst of such holiness and reverent fear You tell me not to be afraid. You are life, and death has no power over You or those You claim.

Jesus, You are glorified. I worship at Your feet. Let me remember how awesome You are!

What was the main thing the Lord spoke to you or changed in you through this meditation?

Nothing Can Separate Me

ROMANS 8:31B-39

If God is for me, who can be against me? You did not spare Your own Son, but delivered Him up for me, how shall You not with Him also freely give me all things? Who shall bring a charge against God's elect? It is God who justifies. Who is he who condemns? It is Christ who died, and furthermore is also risen, who is even at the right hand of God, who also makes intercession for me. Who shall separate me from the love of Christ? Shall tribulation, or distress, or persecution, or famine, or nakedness, or peril, or sword? As it is written:

"For Your sake we are killed all day long;
We are accounted as sheep for the slaughter." Yet in all these things I am more than a conqueror through You, because You love me. For I am persuaded that neither death nor life, nor angels nor principalities nor powers, nor things present nor things to come, nor height nor depth, nor any other created thing, shall be able to separate me from Your love, O, God, which is in Christ Jesus my Lord.

Sit in silence for a couple of minutes and allow yourself to think about whatever parts of this Scripture stand out to you. When your mind begins to wander, read the Scripture again slowly, and see if anything else grabs your attention or imagination. Repeat until nothing else stands out. Make notes in the space below (or in a separate journal) to record what stands out to you.

Engage the Lord in prayer over the thoughts you have recorded. When you finish, go to the next page.

Pray each of the thoughts below back to the Lord. Take time with each one. If more thoughts come as you pray, write them down, either in the space provided or in a separate journal.

You are for me. You have proven it, and I can trust You. You are really for me!

Jesus, the most precious gift in the universe, was given for me. How amazing! How could I ever doubt Your goodness toward me?

God Himself has chosen and purchased me. Who could change that? I am secure in Your love!

No matter the circumstances I go through, I am a conqueror. Nothing can hinder Your purposes for me. I will overcome because You have overcome.

There is nothing that can change Your love for me or cause it to decrease. You never change. Your love for me never changes!

Father, thank You for Your love shown in Christ Jesus my Lord!

What was the main thing the Lord spoke to you or changed in you through this meditation?

Anointed for Purpose

ISAIAH 61:1-3

THE SPIRIT OF THE LORD GOD IS UPON ME,
BECAUSE THE LORD HAS ANOINTED ME
TO PREACH GOOD TIDINGS TO THE POOR;
HE HAS SENT ME TO HEAL THE BROKENHEARTED,
TO PROCLAIM LIBERTY TO THE CAPTIVES,
AND THE OPENING OF THE PRISON
TO THOSE WHO ARE BOUND;
TO PROCLAIM THE ACCEPTABLE YEAR OF THE LORD,
AND THE DAY OF VENGEANCE OF OUR GOD;
TO COMFORT ALL WHO MOURN,
TO CONSOLE THOSE WHO MOURN IN ZION,
TO GIVE THEM BEAUTY FOR ASHES,
THE OIL OF JOY FOR MOURNING,
THE GARMENT OF PRAISE FOR THE SPIRIT OF HEAVINESS;
THAT THEY MAY BE CALLED TREES OF RIGHTEOUSNESS,
THE PLANTING OF THE LORD,
THAT HE MAY BE GLORIFIED.

Sit in silence for a couple of minutes and allow yourself to think about whatever parts of this Scripture stand out to you. When your mind begins to wander, read the Scripture again slowly, and see if anything else grabs your attention or imagination. Repeat until nothing else stands out. Make notes in the space below (or in a separate journal) to record what stands out to you.

Engage the Lord in prayer over the thoughts you have recorded. When you finish, go to the next page.

Pray each of the thoughts below back to the Lord. Take time with each one. If more thoughts come as you pray, write them down, either in the space provided or in a separate journal.

Your Spirit is upon me. You have anointed me.

I have been sent to encourage the poor, heal broken hearts, and proclaim freedom to captives.

This is the year You have promised—the year every wrong is made right, when all hurt is healed. You have sent me to proclaim Your Kingdom is here.

Comfort me when I mourn. Send me to comfort others. Give me joy. Let me release joy.

Father, clothe me with praise so that this dim, colorless spirit of heaviness will be replaced with Your marvelous light.

I am a tree of righteousness—Your planting, that You may be glorified. I bring You glory.

What was the main thing the Lord spoke to you or changed in you through this meditation?

The Winter Is Past

SONG OF SOLOMON 2:10-14

MY BELOVED SPOKE, AND SAID TO ME:
"RISE UP, MY LOVE, MY FAIR ONE,
AND COME AWAY.
FOR LO, THE WINTER IS PAST,
THE RAIN IS OVER AND GONE.
THE FLOWERS APPEAR ON THE EARTH;
THE TIME OF SINGING HAS COME,
AND THE VOICE OF THE TURTLEDOVE
IS HEARD IN OUR LAND.
THE FIG TREE PUTS FORTH HER GREEN FIGS,
AND THE VINES WITH THE TENDER GRAPES
GIVE A GOOD SMELL.
RISE UP, MY LOVE, MY FAIR ONE,
AND COME AWAY!

"O MY DOVE, IN THE CLEFTS OF THE ROCK,
IN THE SECRET PLACES OF THE CLIFF,
LET ME SEE YOUR FACE,
LET ME HEAR YOUR VOICE;
FOR YOUR VOICE IS SWEET,
AND YOUR FACE IS LOVELY."

Sit in silence for a couple of minutes and allow yourself to think about whatever parts of this Scripture stand out to you. When your mind begins to wander, read the Scripture again slowly, and see if anything else grabs your attention or imagination. Repeat until nothing else stands out. Make notes in the space below (or in a separate journal) to record what stands out to you.

Engage the Lord in prayer over the thoughts you have recorded. When you finish, go to the next page.

Pray each of the thoughts below back to the Lord. Take time with each one. If more thoughts come as you pray, write them down, either in the space provided or in a separate journal.

You speak to me. You call to me. You invite me to come away with You.

The winter season is past, the rain is gone, and springtime is here. It is time to sing.

Everything comes alive when I realize how much You love me. I come alive.

The fruit of intimacy is beginning to ripen. Your love is making everything new. Let me set aside time and space to come away with You. I long for You!

I want to see Your face. I want to hear Your voice. Speak, Lord! Your servant is listening.

Jesus, Your wounds are the clefts of the rock. As I stand in the reality of Your broken body, I see how glorious You are!

What was the main thing the Lord spoke to you or changed in you through this meditation?

I Am a Partaker of the Divine Nature

2 PETER 1:2-8

GRACE AND PEACE BE MULTIPLIED TO ME IN THE KNOWLEDGE OF GOD AND OF JESUS MY LORD, AS YOUR DIVINE POWER HAS GIVEN TO ME ALL THINGS THAT PERTAIN TO LIFE AND GODLINESS, THROUGH THE KNOWLEDGE OF YOU WHO CALLED ME BY GLORY AND VIRTUE, BY WHICH HAVE BEEN GIVEN TO ME EXCEEDINGLY GREAT AND PRECIOUS PROMISES, THAT THROUGH THESE I MAY BE A PARTAKER OF THE DIVINE NATURE, HAVING ESCAPED THE CORRUPTION THAT IS IN THE WORLD THROUGH LUST.

BUT ALSO FOR THIS VERY REASON, GIVING ALL DILIGENCE, I WILL ADD TO MY FAITH VIRTUE, TO VIRTUE KNOWLEDGE, TO KNOWLEDGE SELF-CONTROL, TO SELF-CONTROL PERSEVERANCE, TO PERSEVERANCE GODLINESS, TO GODLINESS BROTHERLY KINDNESS, AND TO BROTHERLY KINDNESS LOVE. FOR IF THESE THINGS ARE MINE AND ABOUND, I WILL BE NEITHER BARREN NOR UNFRUITFUL IN THE KNOWLEDGE OF MY LORD JESUS CHRIST.

Sit in silence for a couple of minutes and allow yourself to think about whatever parts of this Scripture stand out to you. When your mind begins to wander, read the Scripture again slowly, and see if anything else grabs your attention or imagination. Repeat until nothing else stands out. Make notes in the space below (or in a separate journal) to record what stands out to you.

Engage the Lord in prayer over the thoughts you have recorded. When you finish, go to the next page.

Pray each of the thoughts below back to the Lord. Take time with each one. If more thoughts come as you pray, write them down, either in the space provided or in a separate journal.

Knowing You brings grace and peace. Knowing You carries promise. That promise is my path to partaking in the divine nature.

It is Your power that gives me what I need to live a life of godliness. Because of Your nature, I look like You.

Lust and sin corrupt. Your power has set me free from that lust and sin. Because of that I give all diligence...

I will be diligent (earnest, striving) to add to my faith virtue (moral excellence), knowledge (a deeper, more perfect understanding), self-control (mastering my own desires and sensual appetites), perseverance (not swerved from my deliberate purpose), godliness (piety), brotherly kindness (cherishing other believers), and love (affection, goodwill, benevolence).

I want to bear fruit in my understanding and experience of who You are.

Lord, all of this is Your work in me. I choose to enter Your rest, trusting Your divine nature in me.

What was the main thing the Lord spoke to you or changed in you through this meditation?

I Will Do Greater Works Through the Love Jesus Shows Me

JOHN 14:11–18

BELIEVE ME THAT I AM IN THE FATHER AND THE FATHER IN ME, OR ELSE BELIEVE ME FOR THE SAKE OF THE WORKS THEMSELVES.

MOST ASSUREDLY, I SAY TO YOU, SINCE YOU BELIEVE IN ME, THE WORKS THAT I DO YOU WILL DO ALSO; AND GREATER WORKS THAN THESE YOU WILL DO, BECAUSE I GO TO MY FATHER. AND WHATEVER YOU ASK IN MY NAME, THAT I WILL DO, THAT THE FATHER MAY BE GLORIFIED IN THE SON. IF YOU ASK ANYTHING IN MY NAME, I WILL DO IT.

IF YOU LOVE ME, KEEP MY COMMANDMENTS. AND I WILL PRAY THE FATHER, AND HE WILL GIVE YOU ANOTHER HELPER, THAT HE MAY ABIDE WITH YOU FOREVER—THE SPIRIT OF TRUTH, WHOM THE WORLD CANNOT RECEIVE, BECAUSE IT NEITHER SEES HIM NOR KNOWS HIM; BUT YOU KNOW HIM, FOR HE DWELLS WITH YOU AND WILL BE IN YOU. I WILL NOT LEAVE YOU ORPHANS; I WILL COME TO YOU.

Sit in silence for a couple of minutes and allow yourself to think about whatever parts of this Scripture stand out to you. When your mind begins to wander, read the Scripture again slowly, and see if anything else grabs your attention or imagination. Repeat until nothing else stands out. Make notes in the space below (or in a separate journal) to record what stands out to you.

Engage the Lord in prayer over the thoughts you have recorded. When you finish, go to the next page.

Pray each of the thoughts below back to the Lord. Take time with each one. If more thoughts come as you pray, write them down, either in the space provided or in a separate journal.

I believe that You are in the Father and the Father is in You. I believe You are One with the Father.

Show me the greater works. What greater works do You have for me to do?

I want to move in power and authority so that the Father will be glorified in Jesus.

I do love You, Lord. I will keep Your commandments!

Thank You for sending me the Helper, the Holy Spirit, to remain in me forever!

Holy Spirit, Your presence in me proves that I am a child of God. I am not an orphan. Speak this truth within me.

What was the main thing the Lord spoke to you or changed in you through this meditation?

Don't Worry—
Just Seek the Kingdom

Matthew 6:25-33

Therefore I say to you, do not worry about your life, what you will eat or what you will drink; nor about your body, what you will put on. Is not life more than food and the body more than clothing? Look at the birds of the air, for they neither sow nor reap nor gather into barns; yet your heavenly Father feeds them. Are you not of more value than they? Which of you by worrying can add one cubit to his stature?

So why do you worry about clothing? Consider the lilies of the field, how they grow: they neither toil nor spin; and yet I say to you that even Solomon in all his glory was not arrayed like one of these. Now if God so clothes the grass of the field, which today is, and tomorrow is thrown into the oven, will He not much more clothe you, O you of little faith?

Therefore do not worry, saying, "What shall we eat?" or "What shall we drink?" or "What shall we wear?" For after all these things the Gentiles seek. For your heavenly Father knows that you need all these things. But seek first the Kingdom of God and His righteousness, and all these things shall be added to you.

Sit in silence for a couple of minutes and allow yourself to think about whatever parts of this Scripture stand out to you. When your mind begins to wander, read the Scripture again slowly, and see if anything else grabs your attention or imagination. Repeat until nothing else stands out. Make notes in the space below (or in a separate journal) to record what stands out to you.

Engage the Lord in prayer over the thoughts you have recorded. When you finish, go to the next page.

Pray each of the thoughts below back to the Lord. Take time with each one. If more thoughts come as you pray, write them down, either in the space provided or in a separate journal.

Picture yourself on a hillside with hundreds of people around you as Jesus speaks those words. Imagine Him looking into your eyes and speaking directly to you. Receive the peace that comes from knowing you are cared for.

Father, I believe that You care for me and that You will provide for me. Forgive me for doubting.

Temporary things receive care from You. How much more will I, the child You gave everlasting life, receive from You?

I am free to seek after Your Kingdom and Your righteousness because You take care of me.

In the seeking of Your Kingdom, everything else is taken care of. Help me to trust in You and Your ways!

I am not an orphan begging—I am a child trusting. I can go about Your business because You take care of mine.

What was the main thing the Lord spoke to you or changed in you through this meditation?

Restore Me, O God!

HAVE MERCY UPON ME, O GOD,
ACCORDING TO YOUR LOVINGKINDNESS;
ACCORDING TO THE MULTITUDE OF YOUR TENDER MERCIES,
BLOT OUT MY TRANSGRESSIONS.
WASH ME THOROUGHLY FROM MY INIQUITY,
AND CLEANSE ME FROM MY SIN.
FOR I ACKNOWLEDGE MY TRANSGRESSIONS,
AND MY SIN IS ALWAYS BEFORE ME.
AGAINST YOU, YOU ONLY, HAVE I SINNED,
AND DONE THIS EVIL IN YOUR SIGHT—
THAT YOU MAY BE FOUND JUST WHEN YOU SPEAK,
AND BLAMELESS WHEN YOU JUDGE.
BEHOLD, I WAS BROUGHT FORTH IN INIQUITY,
AND IN SIN MY MOTHER CONCEIVED ME.
BEHOLD, YOU DESIRE TRUTH IN THE INWARD PARTS,
AND IN THE HIDDEN PART YOU WILL MAKE ME TO KNOW WISDOM.
PURGE ME WITH HYSSOP, AND I SHALL BE CLEAN;
WASH ME, AND I SHALL BE WHITER THAN SNOW.
MAKE ME HEAR JOY AND GLADNESS,
THAT THE BONES YOU HAVE BROKEN MAY REJOICE.
HIDE YOUR FACE FROM MY SINS,
AND BLOT OUT ALL MY INIQUITIES.
CREATE IN ME A CLEAN HEART, O GOD,
AND RENEW A STEADFAST SPIRIT WITHIN ME.
DO NOT CAST ME AWAY FROM YOUR PRESENCE,
AND DO NOT TAKE YOUR HOLY SPIRIT FROM ME.
RESTORE TO ME THE JOY OF YOUR SALVATION,
AND UPHOLD ME BY YOUR GENEROUS SPIRIT.
THEN I WILL TEACH TRANSGRESSORS YOUR WAYS,
AND SINNERS SHALL BE CONVERTED TO YOU.

Sit in silence for a couple of minutes and allow yourself to think about whatever parts of this Scripture stand out to you. When your mind begins to wander, read the Scripture again slowly, and see if anything else grabs your attention or imagination. Repeat until nothing else stands out. Make notes in the space below (or in a separate journal) to record what stands out to you.

Engage the Lord in prayer over the thoughts you have recorded. When you finish, go to the next page.

Pray each of the thoughts below back to the Lord. Take time with each one. If more thoughts come as you pray, write them down, either in the space provided or in a separate journal.

Your goodness comes not because I deserve it but according to Your mercy.

Father, not only forgive me—wash me. Completely remove sin from me. Set me free.

My sin is against You and You alone. I was born Your enemy, yet You forgive me and cleanse me again and again. Such kindness is beyond my understanding.

You want truth deep within me, in my soul. Create a clean heart in me. You want wisdom in my hidden parts, in my spirit. Renew a steadfast spirit in me.

Only You can make my heart clean and brand new—as if I had never sinned. Please do this, God!

Give me Your Spirit. Your salvation is amazing! I am so full of joy that I overflow in praise about You to others!

What was the main thing the Lord spoke to you or changed in you through this meditation?

Notes:

CHAPTER 1

McCambly, R. (2014) Old Testament and Philosophy. *The Lectio Divina* Homepage. Retrieved March 1, 2014, from http://www.lectio-divina.org.

CHAPTER 2

Smithers, D. (2014) The Man with Calloused Knees. *Awaken and Go.* February 20, 2014, from http://www.awakeandgo.com.

CHAPTER 4

Guyon, M. (2011) *Autobiography of Madame Guyon (Authentic Original Classic)* Shippendburg, PA: Destiny Image Publishers.

CHAPTER 6

Bonar, A. (1894) *Andrew A. Bonar, D.D., Diary and Letters.* Paternoster Row, London: Hodder and Stoughton.

CHAPTER 8

Bonar, A. (1894) *Andrew A. Bonar, D.D., Diary and Letters.* Paternoster Row, London: Hodder and Stoughton.

CHAPTER 9

Benge, J & G. (2001) *Christian Heroes: Then & Now, Count Zinzendorf: Firstfruit.* Seattle, WA: YWAM Publishing.

CHAPTER 10

Whaling, F. (1981) *John and Charles Wesley: Selected Prayers, Hymns, Journal Notes, Sermons, Letters and Treatises (Classics of Western Spirituality)* Mahwah, NJ: Paulist Press.

CHAPTER 11

Renquist, T. A. (2000) *Topsy-Turvy Living in the Biblical World: Gospel Sermons for Sundays After Pentecost.* Lima, OH: CSS Publishing Company, Inc.

Notes Continued:

CHAPTER 16

Smithers, D. (2014) About George Fox. *God's Refreshing.* February 20, 2014, from http://networkedblogs.com.

CHAPTER 20

Kendall, R. T. (2011) *Did You Think To Pray: How to Listen and Talk to God Every Day About Everything.* Lake Mary, FL: Charisma Media.

CHAPTER 24

Shorter, K. (June 2, 2012) Prayer Coach. *Prayer Quotes – Madame Guyon.* Retrieved March 1, 2014, from http://prayer-coach.com.

About the Author

JOHN PAUL JACKSON

Recognized as a minister who reveals God, awakens dreams, and leads people closer to Jesus, John Paul Jackson has been an authority on biblical dream interpretation for over thirty years. He renews passion in people of various faiths and age groups with his sincere explanations of the unexplainable mysteries of life and enables people to relate to God and others in fresh and meaningful ways.

As an inspirational author, speaker, teacher of true spirituality, and host of the television program *Dreams & Mysteries*, John Paul has enlightened thousands of people across the world. He finds satisfaction in his role as a youth mentor and advisor to church and national leaders, as well as in the promotion of the spiritual arts.

@JohnPaulJackson
Facebook.com/JPJFanPage
StreamsMinistries.com

About the Contributing Author

JOHN E. THOMAS

 John and his wife, Dawna, were radically saved and delivered and have a desire to see others transferred out of the dominion of darkness into the Kingdom of His wonderful light. They were mentored and ordained by John Paul Jackson, founder of Streams Ministries. They pastored the Metrowest Bridge Church in Natick, Massachusetts, from March 2006 to October 2011. They also founded Life Empowerment to teach and equip the Bride to fulfill her call to represent and reproduce for her King. John currently travels extensively in the United States and Europe accomplishing this mandate.

Facebook.com/JTlifeempowerment
LifeEmpowerment.com

CLASS IS IN SESSION!
WITH JOHN PAUL JACKSON'S
ONLINE CLASSROOM

Take any of our six university-caliber courses written by John Paul Jackson. It's never been easier to take a quantum leap forward in your spiritual walk. Each of these 23-hour courses can be streamed right to your computer, tablet, or smartphone.

Begin your journey to understand all God has for you by going to StreamsMinistries.com. Click on "Online Classroom."

Other Books by
John Paul Jackson

Most of these titles are also available for your e-reading devices. Just search "John Paul Jackson."

Printed in Great Britain
by Amazon

51642467R00108